Alexander Fraser

The Clan Fraser in Canada

Souvenir of the first Annual Gathering, Toronto, May 5th, 1894

Alexander Fraser

The Clan Fraser in Canada
Souvenir of the first Annual Gathering, Toronto, May 5th, 1894

ISBN/EAN: 9783337059408

Printed in Europe, USA, Canada, Australia, Japan

Cover: Foto ©ninafisch / pixelio.de

More available books at **www.hansebooks.com**

THE

CLAN FRASER

IN CANADA

Souvenir

of the

First Annual Gathering

Toronto, May 5th, 1894.

BY

ALEXANDER FRASER

(MAC-PHIONNLAIDH)

TORONTO:
MAIL JOB PRINTING CO.
1895.

Prefatory Note

THE chief object aimed at by the publication of this little volume is to furnish, in a concise and inexpensive form, information regarding the Clan Fraser not readily accessible to clansmen in Canada. It is also hoped a perusal of the contents will strengthen the clan sentiment, and deepen the interest in the ancient clan bond and in the long and illustrious history of the Clan. But the book being essentially an account of the first Annual Gathering held by the Clan in the Province of Ontario, it will be an interesting souvenir of that pleasant event ; and probably the hope may not be too sanguine that its appearance will mark an onward step in the record of the Clan in the Dominion.

The publication has been undertaken under the auspices of the newly-formed Clan Fraser in Canada, and the thanks of the editor are due to Professor W. H. Fraser, of Toronto University, and to Mr. Alexander Fraser (of Fraserfield, Glengarry), the Printing Committee of the Clan; also to Mr. J. Lewis Browne, for the music to which the "Fraser Drinking Song," written by Mrs. Georgina Fraser-Newhall, has been set.

A. F.

Toronto, February, 1895.

Contents.

	PAGE
Introduction	9
Fraser's Highlanders	11
Seventy-First Regiment	15
Fraser De Berry's Organization	16
Formation of the Clan Fraser in Canada	21
First Annual Clan Dinner	22
Toast of "The Clan," containing references to:—	
Origin of the Clan, Change of Surnames	31
Origin of the Name "Fraser"—The Norman-French Theory	37
Mr. Skene's Position Criticised	39
The Bond between Lord Lovat and the Marquis de la Frezelière	40
Scottish Origin of the Name	42
Mr. Homer Dixon's Argument	43
The Frasers in the Lowlands	45
The Clan Fraser Established in the Highlands	49
Succession of the Chiefs	50
Alexander of Beaufort	56
Succession of the Strichen Family	58
A Curious Prediction	59
Reply to the Toast	62
A Guest Honored	65
Toast of "The Clan in Canada."	67
"Distinguished Clansmen"	73
In Art	74
In Science	76
In Literature	81
In Theology	87
In War	88
In Politics	90
Organization of the Clan	92
Georgina Fraser-Newhall	93
Fraser's Drinking Song	96
Simon Fraser, Discoverer of the Fraser River	98
Simon Lord Lovat, Beheaded on Tower Hill	103
Brigadier Simon Fraser	104
Second Annual Dinner	107
Constitution and By-laws of the Clan	110
List of Officers	112
Illustrations:	
Frontispiece—Armorial Bearings of the Clan	
Menu and Toast List Card	23
Alexander Fraser (MacFhionnlaidh)	33
Robert Lovat Fraser	63
Ex-Mayor John Fraser	75
William A. Fraser	79
Georgina Fraser-Newhall	94
Simon, Fourteenth Lord Lovat	102
Brigadier Simon Fraser	105

Introductory

THE Gael has proved himself not less a pioneer of civilization, and adaptable to changing conditions of living, than a lover of the traditions of his race, holding tenaciously by ancient usages and manners, and stirred profoundly by racial sentiment. As a pioneer he has reached " the ends of the earth," possessing the unoccupied parts of the world. As a patriot he has established not a few of his cherished customs in the land of his adoption. His love of kindred is probably his most notable characteristic; it found embodiment in the clan system, under which his race achieved its greatest triumphs and enjoyed its greatest glories, and the bond of clanship, with its inspiring memories, the true clansman will never disregard. While the clan system, as such, would be impracticable in the British colonies under present-day conditions, even more so than in its old home in the Highlands of Scotland, its spirit lives, leavening the system of government and exercising no small influence in the fusion of heterogeneous elements into new and distinct peoples.

These observations are applicable in a peculiar degree to Canada, where a very large number of clansmen have found a second Highland home. Many of the forests which rang with the clash of the claymore in the struggle for British supremacy, fell afterwards to the axe of the Gaelic settler. His trail lies across the continent, from ocean to ocean. His energy and intelligence have been honorably felt in every walk of life, and his enterprise and skill have done much to develop and upbuild the Dominion. No body of people occupies a more distinguished place in this respect than the Frasers; indeed, even among the clans, no name is more closely identified than that of "Fraser" with the early days of Canada. To tell of their services on the field, in government, in commerce, in the professions, would occupy a large volume, as would a similar story of other clans, and an attempt to do so, in an introductory chapter, would be altogether out of place, but there are a few events of importance to the country in which the Frasers figured to which it will be well to allude with fitting brevity.

Those who hold the Norman theory believe the first of the name of "Fraser" in Scotland, "came over with William the Conqueror," and they ask no better proof of the antiquity of the name. If the early connection of the Clan with Canada be any satisfaction to clansmen there, then it may be stated with truth that the first settlers of the name "came over with Wolfe the Conqueror," and their services were as conspicuous in the military operations conducted by the intrepid young General, who gave his life for his country on the Plains of Abraham, as were those performed by any brave knight, whose name may be found on the roll of Battle Abbey.

The story of Fraser's Highlanders forms one of the most romantic chapters in the annals of the clans, and should the time come when it is fairly and fully given to the world, it will prove a valuable addition to the history of Highland life and of early Canada.

For the part taken by the Clan in the uprising of 1745, Lord Simon was beheaded on Tower Hill and the Fraser estates were forfeited to the Crown. The Master of Lovat appeared at the head of the Clan on the Stuart side ; but, as he was young at the time and had acted by his father's command, he was pardoned, and in 1757, in accordance with the wise, conciliatory policy of Mr. Pitt, he was commissioned to raise a regiment of his clansmen, of which he was appointed Lieutenant-Colonel commanding. In General Stewart's Sketches a brief but interesting account of this, the old Seventy-Eighth Regiment, is given, an extract from which will show the strength of the clan ties then existing, and the high character of the men who were raised on the Lovat territory. General Stewart says : " Without estate, money or influence, beyond that influence which flowed from attachment to his family, person and name, this gentleman (the Master of Lovat), in a few weeks found himself at the head of 800 men, recruited by himself. The gentlemen of the country and the officers of the regiment added more than 700, and thus a battalion was formed of 13 companies of 105 rank and file each, making in all 1,460 men, including 65 sergeants and 30 pipers and drummers." All accounts concur in describing this regiment as a superior body of men ; their character and actions raised the military reputation and gave a favorable impression of the moral virtues of the sons of the mountains. The uniform was the full Highland dress, with musket and broadsword, dirk and sporran of badger's or otter's skin. The bonnet was raised or cocked on one side, with a slight bend inclining down to the right ear, over which were suspended two or more black feathers.

The regiment embarked at Greenock, and landed at Halifax in June, 1757, and followed the fortunes of the war for six years. "On all occasions," says Stewart, "this brave body of men sustained a uniform character for unshaken firmness, incorruptible probity and a strict regard both to military and moral duties." Their chaplain was a man of note as of stature. His name was Robert Macpherson, but he was known in the regiment as *An Caipeal Mor*, being of large physique. He exercised the traditional authority of a Highland minister, and we are told that the men were always anxious to conceal their misdemeanors from him.

The cold climate, it was feared, would prove too severe to the Frasers, who wore the kilt, and an attempt, kindly conceived, no doubt, was made to change the "garb of old Gaul" for the trews. The proposal aroused strenuous opposition ; officers and men opposed the change and finally were successful. The strength of feeling awakened may be judged from the words of one of the soldiers in the regiment : " Thanks to our generous chief, we were allowed to wear the garb of our fathers, and, in the course of six winters, showed the doctors that they did not understand our constitution ; for in the coldest winters our men were more healthy than those regiments that wore breeches and warm clothing." A somewhat amusing anecdote is related of how the Nuns of the Ursuline Convent, where the Frasers were quartered in 1759-60, endeavored to induce Governor Murray to be allowed to provide sufficient raiment for the kilted soldiers, but, of course, without success.

At Louisburg, Montmorenci, Ste. Foye and on the Plains of Abraham, the Frasers distinguished themselves greatly. One of the most eloquent tributes to their prowess was spoken by the Hon. P. J. O. Chauveau, the French-Canadian, at the inauguration in 1855 of the Statue of Bellona sent by Prince Napoleon for the monument erected on the famous battlefield. The French-Canadian historian Garneau, and other writers in whose veins courses the blood of the vanquished at Quebec, have borne generous testimony to their military bearing and good conduct. Garneau writes of the battle of Carillon, 1758: "It was the right of the trench works that was longest and most obstinately assailed; in that quarter the combat was most sanguinary. The British Grenadiers and Highlanders there persevered in the attack for three hours, without flinching or breaking rank. The Highlanders above all, under Lord John Murray, covered themselves with glory. They formed the troops confronting the Canadians, their light and picturesque costumes distinguishing them from all other soldiers amid the flames and smoke. The corps lost the half of its men, and twenty-five of its officers were killed or severely wounded;" and the genial Le Moine, half Highland and half French, says: "The Frasers of 1759 and of 1775 readily courted danger or death in that great duel which was to graft progress and liberty on that loved emblem of Canada, the pride of its forests—the Maple Tree. If at times one feels pained at the ferocity which marked the conflict and which won for Fraser's Highlanders at Quebec, the name *Les Sauvages d'Ecosse*,* one feels relieved, seeing that the meeting was inevitable, that the sturdy sons of Caledonia, in Levis'

---

* It is but fair to state that Fraser's Highlanders showed no more ferocity than the usages of war justified. There were barbarous atrocities committed, undoubtedly, but for these, the Highlanders were not responsible. A.F.

heroic Grenadiers, did find a foe worthy of their steel. Scotchmen, on the field of Ste. Foye, in deadly encounter with France's impetuous warriors, doubtless acknowledged that the latter were not unworthy descendants of those whom they had helped to rout England's soldiery on the fields of Brangé, Crevant and Verneuil."

At the close of the war many of the officers and men settled in the Provinces of Quebec and Nova Scotia, having obtained their discharge and grants of land in the New World. It was not long ago computed that the descendants of these Highlanders in the Province of Quebec numbered 3,000, but merged in the French-Canadian peasantry to such an extent that even the names have lost their original form. In Nova Scotia the name Fraser flourishes in every township of every county. There have been many accessions to the Clan since the days of the Seventy-Eighth and the Battle of the Plains, but at least four-fifths of those bearing the Clan name in Canada to-day, trace their descent from the victorious clansmen of Cape Breton and Quebec.

On the outbreak of the American War the Royal Highland Emigrants were embodied, and in that regiment, commanded by the gallant Lieut.-Colonel Allan MacLean (son of Torloisk), 300 men who had belonged to Fraser's regiment enlisted. In the interval between the cession of Canada and the American War, the Lovat estates were restored to the Master of Lovat, for his eminent services (the title was kept in abeyance), and he was asked to raise a regiment, the Seventy-First, of two battalions. This he speedily accomplished and soon found himself at the head of a double regiment numbering 2,340 officers and men. They behaved with the highest distinction throughout the war and earned flattering encomiums from the commanding officers. General Stewart, than whom no more competent authority has written of Highland regiments, and but few who have understood Highland character better, whose Sketches have furnished facts to all subsequent writers on the subject, speaks of the Seventy-First, Fraser's Highlanders, thus: "Their moral conduct was in every way equal to their military character. Disgraceful punishments were unknown. Among men religious, brave, moral and humane, disgraceful punishments are unnecessary. Such being the acknowledged general character of these men, their loyalty was put to the test and proved to be genuine. When prisoners, and solicited by the Americans to join their standard and settle among them, not one individual violated the oath he had taken, or forgot his fidelity or allegiance, a virtue not generally observed on that occasion, for many soldiers of other corps joined the Americans, and sometimes, indeed, entered their service in a body." The Seventy-First did not leave many behind as settlers, and the reference to it here is only permissible as illustrating the high character of the Clan, of which the Seventy-Eighth, which left its quota of settlers behind, formed an important part. General Simon Fraser's intimate connection with Canada, as commanding officer of Fraser's Highlanders (1757), and in other interesting respects, may suffice as a reason why a good anecdote of him may be here related. When the Seventy-First mustered at Glasgow, Lochiel was absent, being ill at London. His absence had not, evidently, been explained to his company, for they demurred to embark without their chief; they feared some misfortune had befallen him. General Fraser had a command of eloquent speech and he succeeded in persuading them to embark with their comrades   It is related that while he was speaking in Gaelic to the men, an old Highlander, who had accompanied his son to Glasgow, was leaning on his staff gazing at the General with great earnestness. When he had finished, the old man walked up to him and, with that easy familiar intercourse, which in those days subsisted between the Highlanders and their superiors, shook him by the hand, exclaiming " Simon, you are a good soldier, and speak like a man ; so long as you live, Simon of Lovat will never die ;" alluding to the General's address and manner, which was said to resemble much that of his father, Lord Lovat, whom the old Highlanders knew perfectly

The De Berry Organization.

We have now seen the origin of the Frasers in Canada ; they came in war, but the swords were readily turned into ploughshares, and the arts of peace cultivated with a constancy and success that equalled their intrepidity and valor on the battlefield. Years rolled on, the Clan multiplied and prospered, and, in the course of time, a project was entered upon for the formation of a new Clan Fraser on Canadian soil The leading spirit of the movement was the Hon. John Fraser de Berry, a member for the Legislative Council of the Province of Quebec. A meeting of Frasers was held in response to the following public advertisement :

FRASER CLAN.

The Frasers of the Province of Quebec are respectfully requested to meet at the office of Messrs. Thomas Fraser & Co., at the Lower Town, Quebec, on Saturday, the twenty-fifth day of January, 1868, at ten o'clock a.m., to take into consideration the advisability of organizing the "Clan" for the Dominion of Canada.

	John Fraser de Berry,	A. Fraser,
	A. Fraser, Sr.,	A. Fraser, Jr.,
	J. R. Fraser,	Fred. Fraser,
January 21, 1868.	John Fraser,	J. Fraser.

At this meeting preliminary steps were taken to further the object in view, and another meeting was held on February 8th, 1868, of which the following report has been taken from the *Quebec Mercury*:

At a meeting of the "Frasers" of the Province of Quebec, held at Mrs. Brown's City Hotel, on the 8th February, 1868, Alexander Fraser, Esq., notary, ex-Member for the County of Kamouraska, now resident in Quebec, in the chair; Mr. Omer Fraser, of St. Croix, acting as Secretary.

1. It was unanimously resolved:

That it is desirable that the family of "Frasers" do organize themselves into a clan with a purely and benevolent social object, and, with that view, they do now proceed to such organization by recommending the choice of

A Chief for the Dominion of Canada;

A Chief for each province;

A Chief for each electoral division;

A Chief for each county;

A Chief for each locality and township.

2. That the Chief of the Dominion of Canada be named "The Fraser," and that he be chosen at a general meeting of the Frasers of all the provinces; the said meeting to be held on the second Thursday in the month of May next, at ten o'clock in the forenoon, in such place in the City of Ottawa as will then be designated.

3. That it is desirable that the Chief of the Province of Quebec and the Chiefs of the electoral divisions represented at said meeting be chosen forthwith; and that the Chief elected for this province be authorized and empowered to name the Chiefs for such divisions as are not represented at present, the said selection shall, however, be subject to the

approbation of the Frasers of the division interested, who will make the same known at a meeting to be called without delay, by the Chief of the Province of Quebec, with the view to proceed to the nomination of the Chiefs of counties comprehended in the said division.

4. That Chiefs of counties be obliged to convene also without delay, a meeting by which shall be chosen all the Chiefs of parishes or townships.

5. That it shall be the duty of the Chief chosen for a parish or township to report to the Chief of his county as early as possible, the number of Frasers residing in his parish or township ; and of the Chief of the county in his town, to report to the Chief of his electoral division, who will transmit it, together with his own report, to the Chief of his province ; the said report to contain the number of Frasers in his division, in order that the force of the Clan in each province may be ascertained on the 14th of May next, at the meeting at Ottawa.

6. That it is advisable that the meeting at Ottawa, representing all the Clan, be composed of all its divers Chiefs from the Chiefs of provinces, even to the Chiefs of parishes or townships inclusively, and any other Frasers who may desire to attend at the same.

7. That the above resolutions and the nominations, which are to take place this day, or which may be made hereafter by the Chief of the province, shall be considered as preliminary and temporary, as they are made with the sole object of organizing the Clan, and not to bind in any manner whatever the Frasers, who will be at perfect liberty to reorganize themselves completely anew at the Ottawa meeting.

8. That the Clan shall not be considered to exist until and after the next anniversary or Dominion Day, the first of July next, under such rules and regulations as will be adopted at the meeting at Ottawa ; the Frasers of this meeting protest energetically against any intention, which might be attributed to them, of dictating their will to their namesakes of this province ; they are simply attempting to organize and with a benevolent object, to adopt temporarily the above resolutions the better to attain that end.

9. That the sister provinces of Ontario, Nova Scotia and New Brunswick be respectfully requested to organize themselves, and to send delegates to the meeting at Ottawa, on the fourteenth of May next, that time having been selected because in all probability the parliament will still be in session, and the members may attend the session before dispersing.

10. That all proceedings be respectfully submitted to the " Fraser " family, which is one of the most ancient, one of the most noble, one of the most influential, and one of the most numerous families of the Dominion of Canada.

11. That all the newspapers throughout the Dominion of Canada, who have subscribers of the name of Fraser, are requested to publish the proceedings of this meeting.

After which the meeting proceeded to the nomination of the following officers, who were unanimously elected :

I. To be the Chief of the Province of Quebec :

The Honorable JOHN FRASER DE BERRY, Esquire, one of the members of the Legislative Council of the said Province, etc., being the fifty-eighth descendant of Jules de Berry, a rich and powerful lord (seigneur) who feasted sumptuously the Emperor Charlemange, and his numerous suite, at his castle in Normandy, in the eighth century.

II. For the following electoral divisions:

Lauzon,—THOMAS FRASER, Esquire, farmer, of Pointe Levis.

Kennebec.—SIMON FRASER, Esquire, of St. Croix.

De la Durantaye,—ALEXANDER FRASER, Esquire, farmer, of St. Vallier.

Les Laurentides,—WILLIAM FRASER, Esquire, of Lake St. John, Chicoutimi.

Grandville,—JEAN ETIENNE FRASER, Esquire, Notary.

Green Island Stadacona,—ALEXANDER FRASER, Esquire, Notary, St. Roch, Quebec.

The meeting having voted thanks to the President and Secretary, then adjourned.

ALEX. FRASER,
President.

OMER FRASER,
Secretary.

There was a good response to the call for the general meeting, letters having been sent broadcast over the Dominion. As chief of the Frasers of British North America, the Hon. James Fraser de Ferraline, in the Province of Nova Scotia, was elected. He was a scion of the Ferraline and Gorthlic families of the Clan. One hundred and eleven subordinate chieftains of provinces and districts were elected and Mr. John Fraser de Berry was appointed Secretary to the "New Clan Fraser," as it was called. For various reasons, chief among them being, probably, its elaborate constitution and the intangible purposes for which it was called into existence, the organization did not make satisfactory headway and in the course of not many years it failed to attract any public attention whatever, and ceased to exist. In its brief career it gathered some interesting information about the clansmen. In a report drawn up by the Secretary, De Berry, whose exertions on its behalf were unwearying, it is stated that there were then over 12,000 persons, men, women and children of the name Fraser, some speaking French, not one of whom was a day laborer, or "earning daily wages," but all in comfortable circumstances, many in positions of honour and trust.

FORMATION

OF THE

CLAN FRASER IN CANADA

Although Mr. John Fraser de Berry's scheme failed it was believed that there was room for a less pretentious and more practicable clan organization in Canada. There was little diminution of the clan feeling ; the desire of those having the same origin and name, the same glorious clan history, in common, to enjoy a friendly intercourse, was natural and reasonable, and at length it assumed a practical form. Early in the spring of 1894 a meeting was held in the office of the *Toronto Daily Mail*, at which there were present : Messrs. George B. Fraser, commission agent ; Robert Lovat Fraser, barrister ; Alexander R. Fraser, druggist ; Dr. J. B. Fraser, physician ; Alexander Fraser (of Fraserfield, Glengarry), Secretary to the Boiler Inspection Company ; W. H. Fraser, Professor of Languages at the Toronto University ; W. A. Fraser, civil engineer and contractor ; W. P. Fraser, clerk,

Dominion Bank; Andrew Fraser, commercial traveller; and Alexander Fraser, of the editorial staff of the *Daily Mail*. The last named, descended from the Clan Mhic Fhionnlaidh sept of the Struy Frasers, was appointed chairman of the meeting and Mr. W. A. Fraser, also descended from good Strathglass stock, was appointed Secretary. All agreed that a clan organization ought to be formed and as a first step it was thought well to test the feeling of the clansmen at a family dinner, which it was decided should be held on May 5th, 1894. Those present formed themselves into a committee to make arrangements for holding the dinner and the chairman and secretary of the meeting were appointed chairman and secretary of the committee. Invitations were sent to every member of the Clan in Ontario, Montreal, New York, Buffalo and Detroit, whose name the committee was able to procure, and about three hundred replies were received, in which, without exception, an earnest hope for the success of the proposed organization was expressed. The dinner took place as had been decided upon, on May 5th, 1894, at Webb's Restaurant, Toronto, and an account of the proceedings will now be given.

THE CLAN DINNER.

Although the number that sat around the festive board was much smaller than had been expected, the elements requisite for a successful gathering were strongly in evidence, and, as a matter of fact, the inaugural dinner of the Clan turned out to be a most satisfactory event. Many of the absentees had conveyed good reasons for their absence, and hearty greetings to the assembled company. From a large

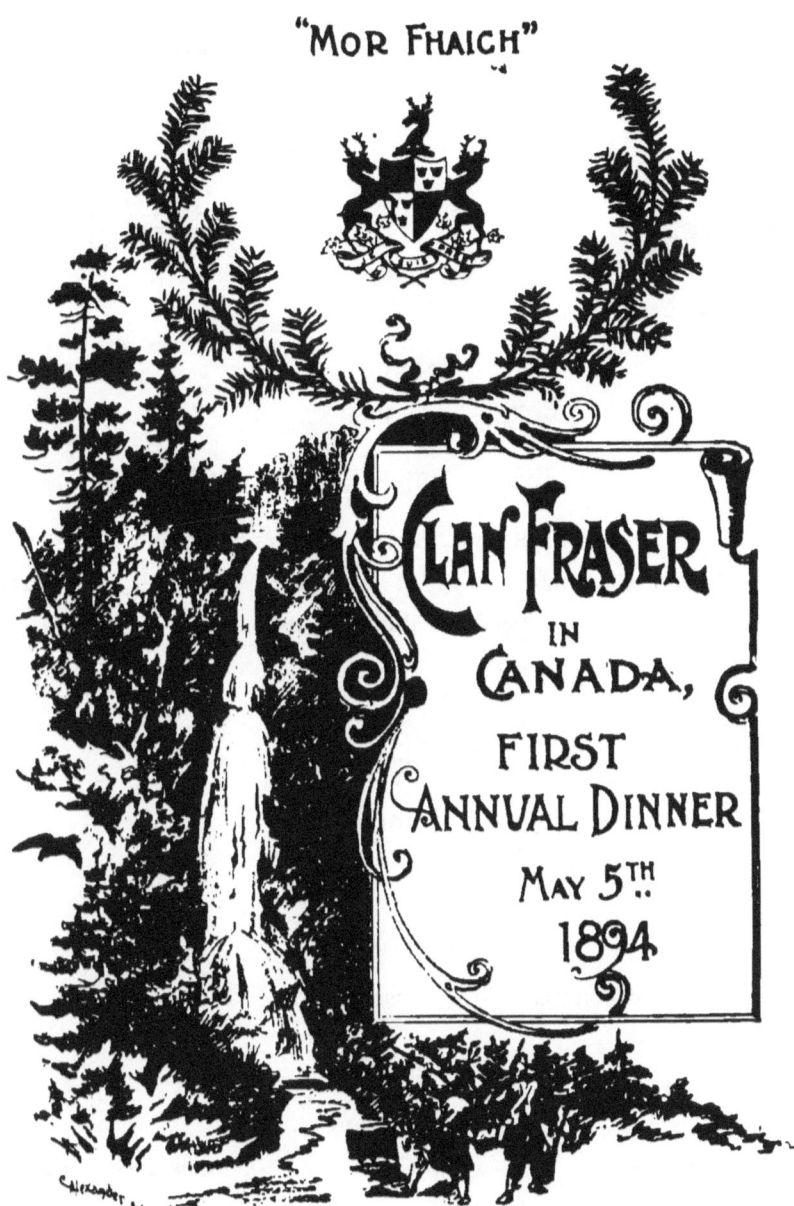

*A chuirm sgaoilte ; chuaias an ceol
Ard sholas a'n tallu nan triath.*—OISEAN.

Menu

Soup.
Scotch Broth.

Fish.
Boiled Sea Salmon from the Cruives of Lovat.

Sgadan beag Poll-a-Roid.   Pomme Natural, Anchovy Sauce.

Bread and Butter Rolled.

Entrees.
HAGGIS
PUNCH A LA ROMAIN.

Joints.
Roast Beef.   Spring Lamb.

Vegetables.
Mashed Potatoes.   Asparagus.   French Peas.

Entremets.
Fraser Pudding.

Curds and Cream.   Oat Cakes.   Assorted Fine Cakes.

Shortbread.   Cheese.   Biscuits.   Radishes.

Neapolitan Ice Cream.   Nuts.   Figs.   Dates.

FRUITS.   COFFEE.

"Smeorach Stratharaigeig: tiseag an urlair."   SEAN-FHOCAL.

Toast List

1. ### The Queen.
   "She wrought her people lasting good."

2. ### The Chief.
   "Tostamaid ar ceann a cinnidh ;
   Mac-Shimi mor na Morfhaich.
   "Master, go on, and I will follow thee
   To the last gasp, with truth and loyalty."
   Bagpipe Music—"Morar Sim."

3. ### The Clan.
   "I tell you a thing sickerly,
   That yon men will win or die ;
   For doubt of deid they sall not flee."
   "'N uair 'thig an cinneadh Frisealach,
   Tha fios gur daoine borb iad"
   Bagpipe Music—"Caisteal Dunaidh."

4. ### Our Guests.
   "Sir, you are very welcome to our house."
   Bagpipe Music—"Aird Mhic-Shimi."
   "Highland Fling," by Master Norman Fraser.

5. ### The Clan in Canada.
   "Kindred alike, where'er our skies may shine,
   Where'er our sight first drank the vital morn."
   Bagpipe Music—"Fhuair Mac-Shimi air ais an Oighearachd."

6. ### Distinguished Clansmen.
   "Of singular integrity and learning,
   Yea, the elect o' the land."
   (a) In Art ; *(b)* in Science ; *(c)* in Literature ;
   (d) in Theology ; *(e)* in War ; *(f)* in Political Life

7. ### The Ladies.
   "Disguise our bondage as we will,
   'Tis woman, woman, rules us still."
   "And when a lady's in the case,
   You know, all other things give place."

8. ### Deoch an Doruis.
   Air (fonn) "Clementine."
   Deoch an doruis, deoch an doruis,
   Deoch an doruis, 's i tha ann ;
   Deoch an doruis, sguab as i,
   Cha'n eil Mac-na-Bracha gann.

Auld Lang Syne.   **God Save the Queen.**

The bagpipe music will be furnished by Mr. Robert Ireland, Pipe Major of the
48th Highlanders, Toronto.

number of letters it would be difficult to make a selection for the reader and the demands of space would prevent it, although some of them are really worth reproducing. Of special interest were the letters from Messrs. O. K. Fraser, Brockville ; John Fraser, Wm. Lewis Fraser and Thomas Fraser, New York ; P. M. Fraser, St. Thomas ; Donald Fraser, Windsor ; R. J. Fraser, Barrie ; R. M. Fraser, Goderich ; Rev. R D. Fraser, Bowmanville ; Rev. J. B. Fraser, M.D., Annan ; John Fraser, Montreal ; W. G. Fraser, Buffalo ; Hon. Christopher Finlay Fraser, and B. Homer Dixon, K.N.L., Toronto ; the last named a Fraser on the maternal side and a gentleman deeply versed in the history of the Clan.

The dining hall presented a very attractive appearance. The table was made beautiful with a tastefully arranged and selected display of flowers and plants, and appropriate to the occasion there were stags' heads on the walls, and the Fraser Clan tartan draped the pillars, doorway and windows. There were a number of articles of interest sent by friends, such as finely executed mezzo-tint pictures of Simon Lord Lovat, beheaded in 1747, and of Brigadier Simon Fraser, the hero of Saratoga ; and a water-color of the Clan arms, from Mr. B. Homer Dixon ; a map of Inverness-shire, showing the Clan possessions at various stages of its history, with the lands in the hands of cadets of the Clan, a life-size copy of Hogarth's picture of Simon Lord Lovat, the "last of the martyrs," a life-size copy of an engraving of Sir Alexander Fraser of Phillorth, founder of the University of Fraserburgh, sent by the Chairman.

The menu card, a copy of which has been reproduced for this volume, will be found to have been a clever effort of the artist, Mr. W. A. Fraser, Secretary of Committee. A representation of the Falls of Foyers is given on the cover, and on the last page a celtic armorial device surrounded by the names of a number of old Fraser estates.

The Chairman was Mr. Alexander Fraser (Mac-Fhionnlaidh); and the vice-chairs were occupied by Mr. Robert Lovat Fraser, Barrister, Toronto, and ex-Mayor Fraser of Petrolea. A picture of the company is given on another page, which will form an interesting reminiscence of the happy gathering. From the picture, the face of one who was present at the dinner is unfortunately absent, that of Mr. Henry Sandham Fraser, and that of Mr. Wm. Fraser, of whom a brief notice is given on another page, appears, although he was not present, as he would have been were it not that he was just then stricken down with illness, to which, not long afterwards, he succumbed. The dinner was excellently served, and then came the toast list with the speeches. The first toast was that of :

"THE QUEEN."

The Chairman in proposing the health of the Queen said :—Our Clan has invariably been a loyal one, even in the rising which terminated so fatally on the battlefield of Culloden, the Clan Fraser took part, believing that they were striking a blow for the rightful king. I am sure we all agree that no sovereign has ever held sway over the British Empire who is more worthy of the regard of men of Highland blood than Her Majesty Queen Victoria. She who has given so many proofs of regard for the Highland people is beloved by them in return. Her volumes of her life in the Highlands, one of which has been well translated into Gaelic and the other indifferently so, bear testimony to the deep interest with which she regards that portion of her ancient kingdom of Scotland, to which we lay claim as our native land. She has gone in and out among the peasantry and gentry with perfect confidence in their loyalty and in their attachment to her person. She surrounded herself by faithful Highlanders, and their services to her, whether in the household or in positions of public preferment, have been uniformly of a high character and invariable success. That she may long live and rule in the hearts of her people, no body of men can wish more strongly than this company that has given to her name its just place of honor at the head of the toast list.

The toast was cordially honored.

"THE CHIEF."

The Chairman next proposed the toast of the Chief. He said: It is stated that a man of the name of Cameron, who had fought at the Battle of Falkirk with the Royal Army, his clan being on the side of the Prince, joined his kinsmen after the battle, but still wore the Royal uniform in the bonnet of which there was a cockade. Lord Kilmarnock, coming up and seeing an armed Royalist, as he thought, suspected danger to the Prince, and in an altercation he snatched the cockade from the soldier's hat and trampled upon it. This aroused the ire of the Camerons who saw their comrade maltreated, and they resented Kilmarnock's interference, saying, " No Colonel nor General in the Prince's army can take that cockade out of the hat of a Cameron except Lochiel himself." I mention this incident as affording a good example of the bond of fealty by which the clansman was held to his chief. To him the chief was supreme in all things. He was not only the head of his family, but the provider and protector of the clan. His authority he derived from his position, his position he secured, sometimes by the good-will of the clan, but generally on account of birth. The clansmen considered themselves as the children of the chief, and the system demanded that they subordinate themselves to his rule. Without a chief or his substitute there could be no organized clan, and it is rightly understood how important was his position under the clan system. Chiefs of our Clan proved themselves to be worthy of the position, as a rule, and Simon Joseph, Lord Lovat, the young nobleman who now holds the chiefship, already gives promise of faithfully following in the footsteps of his forefathers. At the celebration of his majority, not long ago, there was a considerable gathering of clansmen and others to do him honor, and the manner in which he performed his part as host on that occasion is an augury of a distinguished future. It is said that he shows a deep interest in the welfare of his people, that he is a young man of highly patriotic feelings, and, as his sphere of usefulness is a wide one, he, no doubt, will have ample opportunity of filling the highest expectations of the Clan. Following the traditions of his house he has entered the army, and, should he decide to follow arms as a profession, no doubt the military genius of his race, bequeathed to him through a long line of ancestors, will win for him honorable distinction as a soldier. I now ask you to charge your glasses and to drink to the health of our young chief with Highland honors.

The toast was drunk with Highland honors; the company singing "He's a Jolly Good Fellow," after which the piper played the Clan welcome, "Morar Sim."

Mrs. Charles Gordon Fraser was at this stage introduced,

and her little boy, **Master** Norman Fraser, attired in Highland costume, gave a spirited and clever execution of the Highland fling, for which he was enthusiastically cheered.

"THE CLAN."

The Chairman proposed the next toast, that of the Clan. He said:—In rising to propose the toast of the evening, my first duty, it seems to me, is to express my sense of the great honor done me by my clansmen in asking me to preside over the first family dinner of the Clan in this Province. Many there be with us, who, from age and distinction and fitness in every respect, ought to have come before me, and who would have done greater honor to the position on such an occasion as this, than I can hope to do, even with your kind indulgence. The rather active part it has been my privilege to take in bringing about this happy gathering may have suggested your choice, and should I be right in this conjecture, that fact but deepens the feeling with which I regard the honor. But a still more arduous duty laid upon me was to give the toast of the evening, that of "The Clan." I can assure you it required all the courage I could muster to undertake the task. The motto of the Clan was held up to me, but I did not forget that *Je suis prest* ought to be the corollary of *Paratus sum*, and I fear that but few could step into the breach and do full justice to the great Clan Fraser. In assigning the toast, moreover, the request was made that I should give as much information regarding the Clan, as could well be packed into a speech, even if the limit of time should have to be extended over that which is usually allowable for an after dinner effort; but, as I understand the information is intended for a wider circle of clansmen than is here, I feel assured of your patience and forbearance while I struggle through a narrative, the length of which under other circumstances would have been an unpardonable breach of good taste.

The clan system holds an intermediate position between the patriarchal and feudal systems. It is sometimes confused with the former, more rarely with the latter. The feudal lordship, in its genius and scope of operation, was diametrically opposed to the salient characteristics of the clan system. The distinctions need not be enlarged upon here, let it suffice to draw attention to the fact that clanship was a distinct form of government, under well recognized and applied principles. In modern literature we find the characteristic most emphasized to be the loyalty with which the clansman followed and served his chief, as in the words of the quotation on our toast list, " Master, go on and I will follow thee, to the last gasp, with truth and loyalty." That truth and loyalty, however, was not born of a servile, but of a highly patriotic feeling, for the bond which united chief and clansman was that of kindred and common interest, and not of hire and servitude. This explains why a people so highly sensitive, fiery and impetuous as the Celts, gave such loyal and perfect allegiance to the chief of the clan.

Since the fact that we were to hold a clan gathering got abroad, I have been asked for information regarding the origin of the clans in the Highlands. How these clans were first established authentic history does not record with clearness. We are left in the task of unravelling the origin of the clans to meagre allusions in classical writings, in genealogies which, to some extent at least, are mythical, and to tradition, ever changing with the progress of the centuries. There can be no question that many of the

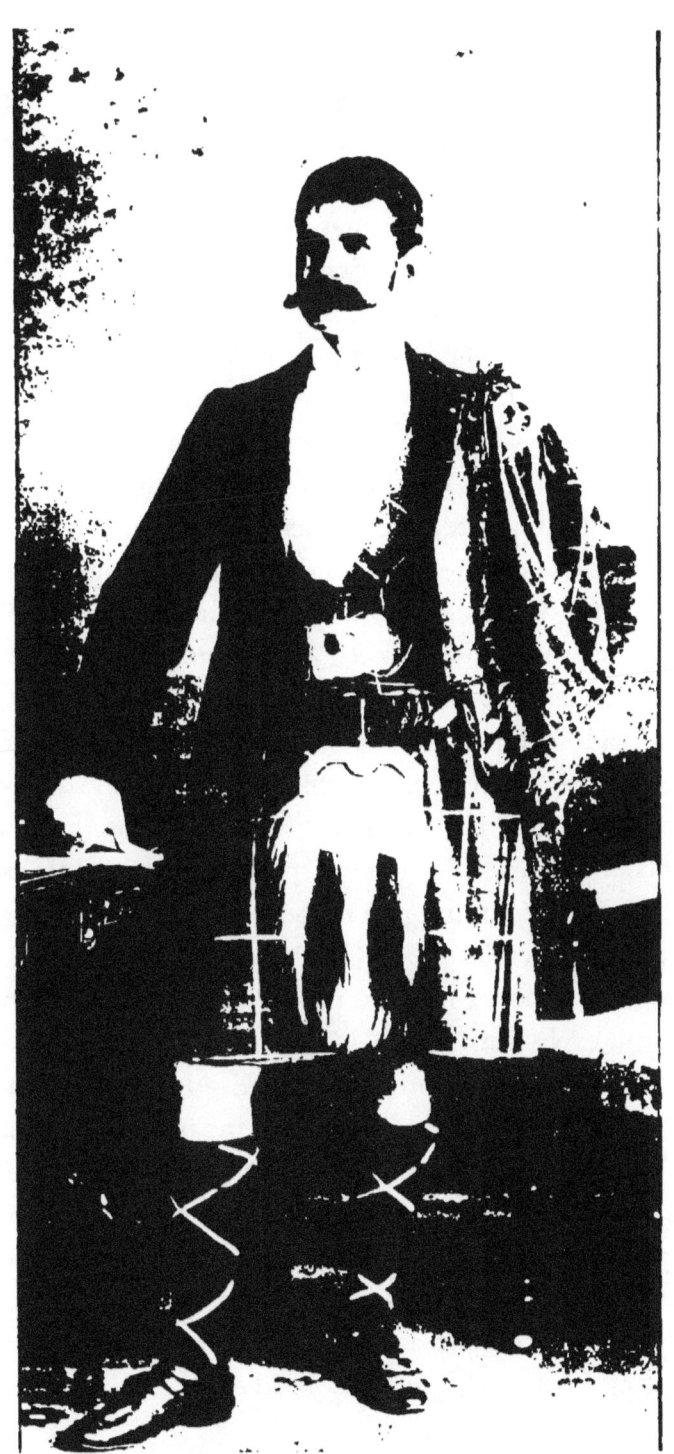

ALEXANDER FRASER (*Mac Fhionnlaidh*),
CHAIRMAN.

clans grew gradually from the native population after the consolidation of the Scottish Kingdom. We know that tribes, some bearing names of modern clans, existed in what may be described as prehistoric times, in the ordinary acceptation of that term, in that part of Scotland north of the Forth and Clyde. Amongst these were the Bissets, the Fentons of the Aird, and others, whose names still survive in the County of Inverness, and who must have to some extent merged into the Fraser Clan, by adopting the name of the lord of the manor. I do not like to quote John Hill Burton as an authority, prejudiced, as he manifestly is, and unfair, as a rule, when dealing with the Highlands and the Celts, but a passage from his unreliable Life of Simon, Lord Lovat, will show how a surname may impose itself on a community and how clans have been, to some extent, constituted. He says: "In some instances the foreign family adopted a purely Celtic patronymic from the name of the sept of which they were the leaders. In other cases, such as the Gordons and Frasers, the sept, probably absorbing various small tribes and admitting to its bosom many stray members owning strange varieties of Gaelic names, took the name of the leader; hence we find the purest Gaelic spoken by people enjoying the Norman names of a Gordon or a Cumin. But, whether the imported lord of the soil adopted the name of the tribe or the tribe that of their lord, the unyielding influence of old national customs and peculiarities prevailed, and their families gradually adapted themselves in speech and method of life to the people over whom they held sway." This principle holds good in the case of the composite Fraser Clan, and a curious example is afforded by an extract from the Allangrange MS., with respect to the Rev. Wm. Fraser, of

Kilmorack, published in that repository of Highland lore, the Celtic Magazine:—

"Bishop Hay, maternal uncle to Agnes Lovat, carried away by Kenneth Mackenzie (a Bhlair), Seventh Baron of Kintail, when he sent away his first wife Margaret, daughter of John, Earl of Ross, advised Kenneth and the lady's friends that a commission should be sent to the Pope in 1491 to procure the legitimation of their union. This was agreed to, and the following is the account of the commissioners:—

"'To that effect one called Donald Dhu McChreggie, priest of Kirkhill, was employed. This priest was a native in Kintail, descended of a clan there called Clan Chreggie, who, being a hopeful boy in his younger days, was educated in Mackenzie's house, and afterwards at Beullie by the forementioned Dugall Mackenzie (natural son of Alexander 'Ionraic' VI. of Kintail pryor yrof). In the end he was made priest of Kirkhill. His successors to this day are called Frasers. Of this priest are descended Mr. William and Mr. Donald Fraser.'

"The author of the Ardintoul MSS. gives a slightly different version, and says: 'To which end they sent Mr. Andrew Fraser, priest of Kintail, a learned and eloquent man, who took in his company Dugald Mackenzie, natural son of Alexander Inrig, who was a scholar. The Pope entertained them kindly, and very readily granted them what they desired, and were both made knights to the boot by Pope Clement VIII., but when my knights came home they neglected the decree of Pope Innocent III. against the marriage and consentricate of the clergy, or, otherwise, they got a dispensation from the then Pope Clement VIII., for both of them married. Sir Dugal was made priest of Kintail and married Nien (daughter) Dunchy Chaim in Glenmoriston. Sir Andrew likewise married, whose son was Donall Dubh MacIntagard (Black Donald, son of the Priest) and was priest of Kirkhill and chapter of Ross. His tacks of the Vicarage of Kilmorack to John Chisholm, of Comar, stands to this day. His son was Mr. William MacAhoulding, *alias* Fraser, who died minister of Kiltarlady. His son was Mr. Donald Fraser, who died minister of Kilmorack ; so that he is the fifth minister or ecclesiastical person in a lineal and uninterrupted succession, which falls out but seldom, and than which, in my judgment, nothing can more entitle a man to be really a gentleman ; for that blood which runs in the veins of four or five generations of men of piety and learning and breeding cannot but have influence, and it confirms my opinion that the present Mr. Wm. Fraser (who is the fifth) has the virtues and commendable properties of his predecessors all united in him.' "

We see here the ease with which a MacCreggie could become a Fraser, and, bearing in mind the principle noticed by Hill Burton, there is no difficulty in accounting for the origin and growth of our Clan in the Highlands. Whether we can tell the day of the month and the year on which Andrew or Simon Fraser first gazed on the winding Beauly or not— and the date can be approximately fixed—we, at all events, have no deep, unfathomable problem to solve as to the formation of the Fraser Clan. We know that the founder of the name in Inverness-shire arrived there as the head of a powerful Lowland house, that he settled among the native Caledonians of the country, assumed possession of the lands then forming his estate ; that the people, who were as Celtic as those in any portion of the Highlands, bearing such names as Gille-Criosd, Mac-Killweralicke, Gill' Aindrea, etc., rallied around him, accepted his authority, became his followers, and gradually adopted the name. As has been remarked, some of those who were thus absorbed were the Bissets and the Fentons of the Aird ; there were also the Haliburtons, the Corbets, and the Graemes of Lovat, whose estates fell into the possession of the Fraser family. From this beginning it is an easy matter to follow the fortunes of the Clan down the centuries from 1296, or thereabout, until the present day. But it is not as easy, nor is it as important, although interesting, to deal with the origin of the name and the ancient seat of those who bore it long, long ago. Yet the theories respecting the origin of the name must be taken notice of as traditions of interest, at least to the Clan.

We meet the name of "Fraser" in various spellings in Ragman Roll, which dates A.D. 1292-97. Seventeen gentlemen of the family are on the roll, and the spellings given are: Fraser, Fresar, Frisel, Frisele, Freshele, de Fraser, and de Frisle. Whence derived? A Norman-French and a Celtic origin have been ascribed to it.

THE NORMAN-FRENCH ORIGIN.—Skene settles this theory in a summary fashion. He accepts it as indubitable, and had he refrained from giving the grounds upon which he bases his opinion, his deservedly high reputation as a Celtic historian might have satisfied the general reader as to the truth of his *ipse dixit*. But the two reasons he advances are absurd. From his own words you will learn how he disposes of the origin of the Clan: "Of the Norman origin of the family of the Frasers it is impossible for a moment to entertain a doubt. They appear during the first few generations uniformly in that quarter of Scotland which is south of the

Firths of Forth and Clyde, and they possessed at a very early period extensive estates in the counties of East Lothian and of Tweeddale; besides the name of Frisale, which is its ancient form, appears in the roll of Battle Abbey, thus placing the Norman character of their origin beyond a doubt." Mr. Skene's first reason is that, " they appear during the first few generations uniformly in that quarter of Scotland which is south of the Forth and Clyde." Had this part of Scotland been at that time inhabited by Normans, Mr. Skene's position would not seem so surprising as it does; but, as a matter of fact, at the time when the Frasers, according to Skene himself, flourished in the south of Scotland, the population there was Celtic, and his plain reasoning is: " The Frasers first appear in Scottish records as part of a Celtic population; therefore they must be of Norman origin!" Mr. Skene's second reason, while not so manifestly absurd, is equally weak. It is: " The name of Frisale, which is the ancient form of " Fraser," appears in the roll of Battle Abbey, thus placing the Norman character of their origin beyond a doubt." And it is on such grounds as these that Mr. Skene proceeds. Why, the ingenious Senachies, skilled in genealogy, if not in the unravelling of charter deeds, could give an infinitely more plausible statement of a continental descent. In the first place, it is now impossible to authenticate the genuineness of the Roll of Battle Abbey; and in the second place, if the roll were beyond question, there is nothing to show that the Frisale whose name appears on it was the progenitor of the Scottish Frasers. Mr. Skene does not pretend to prove that he passed from England to Scotland and founded the family there. But although he does not give us details, Mr. Skene's theory can be nothing else than that Frisale, the follower of

William the Conqueror, was the same who received the lands held by the family in 1109 in the south of Scotland from the Scottish monarch. Let us see how this theory will bear examination. One sentence disposes of it completely and forever. There were Frasers in possession of estates in the south of Scotland before the Battle of Hastings, and from them Gilbert Fraser, who figures in the Cospatrick Charter of 1109, was descended. Long before 1109 the family had possessions in the Lothians and Tweeddale and farther to the north. It requires no more than this statement of fact to dispose of the Roll of Battle Abbey and the Frisale whose name furnished the late Historiographer Royal of Scotland with an easy outlet from an apparently difficult position. But supposing we allow for a moment the prior occupation of the Frasers to disappear from view, and with Skene begin at 1109 with Gilbert Fraser. Even then the case for Frisale would be hopelessly weak. The Battle of Hastings was fought in 1066. From 1058 to 1093 Malcolm Ceanmor sat on the Scottish throne; he it would be, according to Skene, who gave Frisale the grant of the extensive estates of the Tweeddale Frasers. But he was the bitter foe of William the Conqueror, who supplanted Edgar Atheling, whose sister Margaret was Malcom's Queen, and whose nephew, also named Edgar, reigned in Scotland until 1107. Is it credible that Malcolm or Donald Bane, or Duncan, or Edgar, would strip their own nobles, in times of very uncertain warfare, of their lands, in order to bestow them upon aliens, and these aliens the feudal vassals of their turbulent, warlike enemy? No careful reader of that period of Scottish history can believe that to have been possible. If it be said that Alexander I. and David I. favored Norman courtezans with grants of land on feudal titles, the answer is that Alexander mounted the throne not earlier than 1107, when the Frasers had already achieved historic prominence. While these remarks may suffice to indicate how valueless are the reasons put forward by Mr. Skene, they do not touch other theories pointing to a French origin prior to the reign of Malcolm Ceanmor. But these other theories having been rejected by Mr. Skene and his school, we may conclude that they rest their case on the statements just alluded to and disposed of.

Annalists and Clan historians have, however, gone into particulars of the Norman-French theory. According to some the name was derived from the *fraise* or 'strawberry' leaves in their arms, and it was related that they sprang from the Frezels of France. Others give different origins; but, before laying before you the serious objections to the Norman-French theory, it is right that I should repeat what has been in many quarters regarded as strong circumstantial evidence in its favor. I refer to the bond entered into, as late as the first part of the eighteenth century, between Simon Lord Lovat (who was beheaded) and the Marquis de la Frezelière. Lord Lovat was a fugitive in France at the time, and he was befriended by the Marquis. He wrote his life in French, afterwards translated into English and published in 1796. In it he makes the following statement:—

"The house of Frezel, or Frezeau de la Frezelière, is one of the most ancient houses in France. It ascends by uninterrupted filiation, and without any unequal alliance, to the year 1030. It is able to establish by a regular proof sixty-four quarterings in its armorial bearings, and all noble. It has titles of seven hundred years standing in the abbey of Notre Dame de Noyers in Touraine. And it is certain,

that, beside these circumstances of inherent dignity, the house de la Frezelière is one of the best allied in the kingdom. It numbers among its ancestors on the female side daughters of the families de Montmorenci, de Rieux, de Rohan, de Bretagne, de la Savonniere, de la Tremouille, de la Grandiere, and de St. Germains. Through the houses de Montmorenci, de Rieux, de Rohan, and de la Tremouille, to which the Marquis de la Frezelière is nearly allied, he can trace his filiation through all the French monarchs, up to Charlemagne, King of France and Emperor of the West. Down again through the various branches of the illustrious house of France, M. de la Frezelière may, without impropriety, assert his alliance to all the royal houses and almost all the principal nobility of Europe.

"It is demonstrated by various historians, by the tradition of the two families, and from letters written from time to time from one to the other, that the house of Frezel or Frezeau de la Frezelière in France, and the house of Frezel or Fraser in Scotland, were of the same origin, and derived from the same blood. The Marquis de la Frezelière, the head and representative of the Frezels or Frezeaus in France, and Lord Lovat, the representative of the Frezels or Frasers in the north and the Highlands of Scotlands, having happily encountered each other at Paris in the second journey that Lord Lovat made to France for the service of his king (1702), were therefore both of them highly gratified with the opportunity that offered itself of renewing their alliance and declaring their affinity in a common and authentic act of recognition drawn up for that purpose.

"This record was executed on the one part by the Marquis de la Frezelière himself, by the Duke de Luxembourg, the

Duke de Chatillon and the Prince de Tingrie, the three worthy and illustrious children of the late Marshal de Luxembourg Montmorenci, whose heroic exploits are not less glorious and celebrated than his descent is ancient and august. Several other lords of the house of Montmorenci, the Marquis de Rieux, and many noblemen related by blood and marriage to M. de la Frezelière, joined with the Marquis in affixing their signatures to this act of recognition. On the other part it was executed by Simon Lord Lovat, Mr. John Fraser, his brother, and Mr. George Henry Fraser, Major of the Irish regiment of Bourke in the French service, for themselves, in the name of their whole family in Scotland.

"By this deed the kindred of the two houses of the Frezels or Frasers is placed out of all possible doubt. Accordingly from the moment in which it was executed the Marquis de la Frezelière regarded Lord Lovat rather as his brother and his child than as his remote relation ; and had his re-establishment in Scotland nearer his heart than his own elevation in France."

THE SCOTTISH ORIGIN OF THE NAME. —Logan, author of the "Scottish Gael," agrees with those who claim a Scottish origin for the name. He derives it from *Frith*, 'a forest,' and *siol*—'seed,' 'offspring.' His theory has at least the merit of great probability, and is certainly to be preferred to the Norman-French, unless the latter can be supported by better evidence than has yet been brought forward. In a most interesting volume on surnames by Mr. B. Homer Dixon, K.N.L., published in 1857, there are very suggestive notes on the surname "Fraser." He agrees with Logan, and he combats the Norman origin. His interest in the Clan Fraser is one of descent from a notable cadet family, and in connection with the origin of the name he has kindly furnished me with the following valuable statement:—

"I differ from Skene and the older writers who derive the Frasers either from Pierre Fraser, who came to Scotland about the year 800, and whose son Charles was made Thane of Man in 814, or from Julius de Berry, of Averne in the Bourbonnais, who, in the year 916, gave Charles the Simple so delicious a dish of strawberries that the king changed his name to 'de Fraize' and gave him 'fraizes' for arms.

"According to the best authorities hereditary surnames were not used until about the year 1000, and Arms were certainly not borne until after the Norman Conquest, being only introduced about four score years later at the time of the second Crusade, viz., A.D. 1146, and therefore more than two centuries after the date of those ascribed to Julius de Fraize.

"That the last Lord Lovat believed in his Norman descent I do not doubt. Early in the last century (A.D. 1702) he signed a bond of recognition with the Marquis Frezeau or Frezel de la Frezelière, declaring that their name and origin were the same and acknowledging themselves as relations. The Frezeaus, however, were Anjevins from near Saumur, while the first Scotch Fraser was said to be a Bourbonnais; still both parties were probably easily satisfied with their bond, which only went to prove apparently more clearly the antiquity of the families, however unnecessary, for the Frezeaus or Frezels were one of the most ancient houses in France, and the Frasers are undoubtedly one of the noblest families in Scotland. Burton, in his Life of Lord Lovat, London, 147, p. 104, throws discredit upon Lord Lovat's statement (Memoirs of Lord Lovat, London) of the antiquity of the family of Frezeau de la Frezelière, because, forsooth, there is no account of the family in 'le Père Anselme,' but Moreri (Grand Dicte. Histe. Basle. 1740) says ' the family was one of the most ancient in the kingdom ' (almost the very words of Lord Lovat), ' and one of the most illustrious of the Province (Anjou), where they have possessed from time immemorial the seigniory of the Frezelière.' Moreri adds that there were Chevaliers Frezel in 1030, and, commencing his pedigree with the Chevalier Geoffrey, living in 1270, carries it down uninterruptedly to the Marquis de la Frezelière, et de Monsieur Baron de Lasse, Lieutenant-General in the army and first Lieutenant-General in the Artillery, who died in 1711.

" Both the Marquis and Lord Lovat were mistaken, however, for the Anjevin name does *not* signify ' strawberry,' neither does that family bear 'fraises' in their arms, but Frezeau or Frezel de la Frezelière signifies ' Ash of the Ash Plantation or Wood,' from the Romance word *Fraysse*, 'an ash tree ;' and in Auvergne there is a family styled ' du Fraisse,' who bear an ash tree in their arms. Similar names to Frezel de la Frezelière are le Bastard de la Bastardière, Freslon de la Freslonnière, Raband de la Rabandière.

" It is true that the name Frisell occurs in the Roll of Battle Abbey ; but even allowing that to be authentic, what proof is there that the Frisell who accompanied the Conqueror in 1066, was the ancestor of Gilbert de Fraser, who possessed large estates in Tweeddale and Lothian in the time of Alexander I. (1107-1174) ?

" This Gilbert, the first of the family mentioned, is called ' de,' but the name was more frequently written without that prefix.

"I believe that the Frasers are Scotch *ab origine* and repeat that I consider the name to be Gaelic and older than the arms, which were canting arms, such as we have a royal example of as early as the time of Louis VII. (of 1180), who covered the shield of France with blue, the tincture of his royal robes, and then charged the same with lilies, derived originally from Isis, formerly worshipped in France.

"The *fraises* are quartered with three antique crowns, and here again authors differ, most writers saying they are for Bisset. Even Nisbet makes this error, although on another page he gives the arms of Bisset of Beaufort as 'Azure a bend argent!' Others say they were granted to Sir Simon Fraser, the 'Flower of Chivalrie,' the friend of Wallace and Bruce, for having three times re-horsed his king at the Battle of Methven, in 1306. This *may* be their origin, but if so they were probably granted to or adopted by his grand nephew and heir, Sir Andrew Fraser, for Sir Simon Fraser was taken prisoner at this very battle, conveyed to London and beheaded. It is worthy of note, however, that the Grants, near neighbors and often allied to the Frasers, bear three antique crowns, though of a different tincture. Hugh, fifth Lord Lovat, married a daughter of the Laird of Grant, by whom, however, he had no issue. He died 1544."

In another note Mr. Dixon says: "The court language of Scotland, at the time this family took their arms, which are totally different from those of the French house of Frezeau or Frezel, was a medley of Teutonic and French."

IN THE LOWLANDS OF SCOTLAND.—But whether the derivation be from the Romance *fraysse*, 'an ash tree,' or the Gaelic *frith*, 'a forest,' we find the chief of the name firmly established as a powerful Scottish noble, manifesting the patriotism and national sentiment to be looked for in a native born baron, as early as 1109.

His name was GILBERT DE FRASER, who, in the year named, witnessed a charter known as the Cospatrick Charter. It is generally conceded that he is the first with whom documentary history begins. That there were Frasers in Tweeddale and Lothian before him is certain, and the names of some of them have survived, but with this Gilbert begins the unbroken record of lineage which comes down to our own day. The lands possessed by the Frasers in the south of Scotland were extensive, and the family power was great, as will be indicated in the course of the brief reference to it which will be here made. Gilbert had three sons, Oliver, Udard and another whose name is not now known.

OLIVER succeeded his father and built Oliver Castle, by which his name survives. There are many interesting descriptions of this old stronghold; that in the Ordnance Survey Report I quote on account of its brevity: "An ancient baronial fortalice in Tweedsmuir parish, S. W. Peeblesshire, on the left side of the river Tweed... Crowning a rising ground which now is tufted with a clump of trees, it was the original seat of the Frasers, ancestors of the noble families of Lovat and Saltoun, and passed from them to the Tweedies, who figure in the introduction to Sir Walter Scott's *Betrothed*, and whose maternal descendant, Thomas Tweedie-Stodart (b. 1838; suc. 1869), of Oliver House, a plain modern mansion hard by, holds 1144 acres in the shire... Oliver Castle was the remotest of a chain of strong ancient towers, situated each within view of the next all down the Tweed to Berwick, and serving both for defence and for beacon fires in the times of the border forays. It was eventually relinquished and razed to the ground." Oliver died without issue, and, his brother Udard, evidently having predeceased him, the succession went to Udard's son,

ADAM, who was succeeded by his son,

LAWRENCE, on record in 1261, and who was in turn succeeded by his son,

LAWRENCE. The second Lawrence had no male issue, but had two daughters, one of whom married a Tweedie, carrying with her Fraser lands, and the other of whom married a Macdougall. The succession in the male line now reverted to Gilbert's third son, whose name is lost, but who had two sons,

SIMON and Bernard. Both these succeeded to the chiefship, Simon's issue being female. It was after this Simon that Keith-Simon was named.

BERNARD raised the fortunes of the family considerably, and his name frequently occurs in connection with questions of first class importance. He was the first of the name to have been appointed Sheriff of Stirling. He was succeeded by his son,

GILBERT, styled " Vicecomes de Traquair," or Sheriff of Traquair, father of three historic personages, Sir Simon, Sir Andrew, and William, the Bishop of St. Andrew's and Chancellor of Scotland, an extended reference to whom I with difficulty refrain from making. As a prelate and a statesman he rendered high service to his country. His brother,

SIR SIMON, THE ELDER, succeeded his father, Gilbert. He is designated the Elder to distinguish him from his famous son, Sir Simon the Patriot. He took a leading part in the affairs of the nation. He, his two brothers and a nephew,

Richard Fraser, Lord of Dumfries, were four of the arbiters in the Baliol claim to the Scottish Crown. He died in 1291, and was succeeded by

Sir Simon the Patriot, the greatest and most renowned of all the Fraser chiefs. All I can say of him is that he was the compatriot, the coadjutor and compeer of Sir William Wallace, and one of the noblest knights whose deeds are recorded on the page of history. He has furnished ancient and modern historians with a subject for patriotic eulogy and enthusiastic praise. As a soldier and statesman he was *facile princeps*. He was the hero of Roslin: he was the only Scottish noble who held out to the last with Sir William Wallace, and was one of the first to welcome and aid the Bruce, whom he re-horsed three times at the Battle of Methven, where he was taken prisoner; and he was the only Scottish knight at that time whose patriotism entitled him to the brutal indignities of Edward's court, and a death, in 1306, similar to that of Sir William Wallace. The Patriot's family consisted of two daughters; the elder married Sir Hugh Hay, ancestor of the noble house of Tweeddale, and the younger, Sir Patrick Fleming, ancestor of the Earls of Wigton. Male issue having again failed, the succession went back to

Sir Andrew Fraser, Sheriff of Stirling, already mentioned as second son of Sir Gilbert Fraser, Sheriff of Traquair. Sir Andrew was the Patriot's uncle. He is styled "of Caithness," on account of having married a Caithness heiress, and at that point begins the interest of the family in the North of Scotland. He was both a brave knight and a powerful lord, and, like his brothers, bore his part valorously and well in the senate and on the field. He lived to occupy the position of chief but two years. He was the first chief of the family who won large possessions in the north, while the headquarters were still in the southern countries. The well-known Neidpath castle was one of the family strongholds. It was a massive pile, of great strength, the walls being eleven feet thick. It is situated in Peeblesshire and is still to be seen. The strawberries appear in the crest of the Hays on the keystone of the courtyard archway, a connecting link with the Frasers, from whom it passed to the Hays of Yester, in 1312, with the daughter of the Patriot. Before following the family to the Lovat estates, in Inverness-shire, it may not be amiss to recapitulate the succession in the south. It was as follows :

I. GILBERT DE FRASER, II. OLIVER FRASER, III. ADAM FRASER, IV. LAURENCE FRASER, V. LAURENCE FRASER, VI. SIMON FRASER, VII. BERNARD FRASER, VIII. SIR GILBERT FRASER, IX. SIR SIMON FRASER, X. SIR SIMON FRASER, XI. SIR ANDREW FRASER.

THE CLAN IN THE HIGHLANDS.—The family extended northward by the marriage of Sir Andrew to a Caithness heiress, through which he acquired large estates in that country. His was a notable family of sons. The eldest, named Simon, gave the family its patronymic of " Mac-Shimi" (pronounced Mac-Kimmie). He (Simon) married the daughter of the Earl of Orkney and Caithness, and it is believed by the family historians that this marriage brought the first Lovat property to the family. It would appear that the Countess of Orkney and Caithness, namely, Simon Fraser's mother-in-law, was the daughter of Graham of Lovat, and that her right in the Lovat property descended to her daughter, Simon's wife, in whose right he took possession. Thus, we see how the names Fraser and Lovat, now for so long a time almost synonymous, were first brought together, and how the Frasers obtained a footing on territory which has become indissolubly linked with their name.

Sir Andrew Fraser's other sons were Sir Alexander, Andrew and James; the first named, a powerful baron and statesman, who attained to the office of Chamberlain of Scotland, held previously, as we have seen, by his uncle, Bishop Fraser. In consideration of distinguished services, he was given in marriage Mary, sister of King Robert Bruce, and widow of Sir Nigel Campbell, of Lochow. He possessed lands in Kincardine, of which county he was sheriff. He was killed at the battle of Dupplin. Andrew and James, his brothers, with their brother, Simon of Lovat, were slain at the battle of Halidon Hill, July 22nd, 1333, and all four were in the front rank of the soldiers of their time.

The chiefs of the Clan Fraser date from:

I. SIMON, Sir Andrew's eldest son. He had three sons—Simon and Hugh, who both succeeded him in honors and estates, and James, who was knighted on the occasion of the coronation of Robert III.

II. SIMON succeeded his father, when still very young, and gave proof, in the field, that the military genius of the family was inherited by him. He died unmarried, after a brief but brilliant career, and his estates and the chiefship went to his brother,

III. HUGH, styled "Dominus de Lovat." And, now, I shall keep briefly to the line of chiefs, and shall not burden you with many personal incidents that have come down to us, with respect to any of them, until we come to Lord Simon, who suffered death on Tower Hill. Hugh was succeeded by his two sons, first by ALEXANDER, the eldest, then by Hugh, the second son. From his third son, John, sprang the Frasers of Knock, in Ayrshire; and from Duncan, his fourth son, the Frasers of Morayshire.

IV. ALEXANDER is described as a "pattern of primitive piety and sanctity to all around him." He died unmarried. An illegitimate son, named Robert, was the progenitor of "Sliochd Rob, Mhic a Mhanaich."

V. HUGH, his brother, who succeeded, acquired lands from the Fentons and Bissets, by marriage with the heiress of Fenton of Beaufort. The names of these lands, it will be interesting to note, forming as they do an important part of the estates long held by the Frasers. They are: Guisachan, now the property of Lord Tweedmouth; Comar, Kirkton, Mauld, Wester Eskadale and Uchterach. This Hugh, the fifth chief, was the first to assume the title of Lord Lovat. He had three sons, Thomas, Alexander, who died unmarried, and Hugh. The first Lord Lovat was succeeded by his son,

VI. THOMAS, whose assumption of the title is not mentioned by the family historians, but of whose accession there is good documentary proof. The silence of the historians, however, has led to an error in the designation of his successors. For instance, his brother,

VII. HUGH, who succeeded him, is called Hugh, second Lord Lovat, instead of Hugh, third Lord Lovat. This Lord Lovat had two sons, Thomas and Hugh, the former of whom was Prior of Beauly, and died young and unmarried. He was succeeded by his son,

VIII. HUGH, fourth Lord Lovat, who had a decisive brush with the Macdonalds, under the Lord of the Isles, when the latter besieged the Castle of Inverness in 1429. He was a peer of Parliament, and is supposed to have been the first Lord Lovat to have attained to that dignity, with the title, Lord Fraser of the Lovat. He had four sons, who deserve mention: Thomas, who succeeded; Hugh, a brave soldier and accomplished courtier, who was slain at Flodden; Alexander, from whom sprang the old cadets of Farraline, Leadclune, etc.; and John, the historian of Henry VIII., the learned Franciscan and astute ambassador. There were also two illegitimate sons—Thomas and Hugh, the latter, progenitor of the Frasers of Foyers, and of many other Fraser families, known as "Sliochd Huistein Fhrangaich."

IX. THOMAS, fifth Lord Lovat, added the lands of Phopachy, Englishton, Bunchrew and Culburnie, the last-named place from Henry Douglas, to the family estates, which were assuming very large proportions. He had a large family. The eldest son, named Hugh, succeeded to the estates. From the second son, William, sprang the Frasers of Belladrum, Culbokie, Little Struy, etc.; from James, the Frasers of Foyness; from Robert, the Frasers of Brakie, Fifeshire; from Andrew, "Sliochd Anndra Ruadh a Chnuic" (Kirkhill); from Thomas, "Sliochd Ian 'Ic Thomais"; John married a daughter of Grant of Grant, with issue; and from Hugh Ban of Reelick (an illegitimate son), came the Frasers of Reelick and Moniack.

X. HUGH, sixth Lord Lovat, was the chief of the Clan at the time of the disastrous fight with the Macdonalds at Kinlochlochy, of which I shall read a short description later on.* At this affray Lord Hugh and his eldest son, Simon, were slain. His second son, Alexander, succeeded, and his

*See account by Rev. Allan Sinclair, A. M., in Celtic Magazine.

third son, William, was ancestor of the Frasers of Struy. His fourth son, Hugh, died young and unmarried.

XI. ALEXANDER, seventh Lord Lovat, a man of literary tastes, lived in comparative retirement. His three sons were: Hugh, his successor; Thomas, first of Knockie and Strichen, from whom the present chief, whose family in 1815 succeeded to the Fraser estates, sprang, and James, ancestor of the Frasers of Ardachie, the Memoir and Correspondence of a scion of which, General James Stuart Fraser, of the Madras Army, was a few years ago, given to the world, as the distinguished record of a soldier, a scholar and a statesman.

XII. HUGH, the eighth Lord Lovat, succeeded at the age of fourteen. He was noted for his proficiency in archery, wrestling, and the athletics of the day; he greatly encouraged the practice of manly exercises on his estates. He was a staunch supporter of Regent Murray, and at the Reformation secured possession of the Priory of Beauly and the church lands pertaining to it, including the town lands of Beauly, and some of the best tacks on the low-lying part of the present estates, in the parishes of Kilmorack and Kiltarlity, the mere names indicating the value of the grant: Fanblair, Easter Glenconvinth, Culmill, Urchany, Farley, Craigscorry, Platchaig, Teafrish, Annat, Groam, Inchrorie, Rhindouin, Teachnuic, Ruilick, Ardnagrask, Greyfield, the Mains of Beauly, as well as valuable river fishings. Mr. Chisholm Batten's book on Beauly Priory contains many interesting facts regarding the acquisition of these fertile and extensive lands, for which his Lordship paid a certain sum of money. He married a daughter of the Earl of Athol, and had two sons, Simon and Thomas, and a natural son, named Alexander, who married Janet, daughter of Fraser of Moniack. Thomas died in his ninth year. Lord Hugh died at Towie, in Mar, on his way home from Edinburgh. It was suspected that he had been poisoned.

XIII. SIMON, ninth Lord Lovat, succeeded at the tender age of five. Thomas of Knockie became tutor for the young chief, an office of power and responsibility. He was married three times. By his first wife, Catherine Mackenzie, he had issue, a son and daughter, Hugh, his successor, and Elizabeth. By his second wife, the daughter of James Stuart, Lord Doune, he had two sons and three daughters: Sir Simon of Inverallochy, Sir James of Brea, Anne, Margaret and Jean. His third wife was Catherine Rose of Kilravock.

XIV. HUGH, tenth Lord Lovat, had already a large family when he succeeded to the estates. Three years after his accession his wife died, leaving him with nine children, six sons and three daughters. Her death cast a gloom over his life, and, practically retiring from business, the management of the estates for a time fell on his son Simon, Master of Lovat, a young man of the brightest promise, whose untimely death was a second severe blow to his father. His dying address is a remarkable production. His next elder brother, Hugh, became Master of Lovat, and Sir James Fraser, of Brea, became tutor. The Master of Lovat married Lady Anne Leslie, and died a year afterwards, during his father's lifetime, leaving a son, Hugh, who succeeded to the titles and estates. Hugh the tenth Lord Lovat's issue were: Simon and Hugh, to whom reference has just been made; Alexander, who became tutor; Thomas of Beaufort, father of the celebrated Simon; William, who died young; James, who died without issue, and Mary, Anne and Catherine.

XV. HUGH, grandson of the tenth Lord Lovat, succeeded

as eleventh Lord Lovat, when only three years old. At sixteen he was, to use the words of the chronicler, " decoyed into a match " with Anne, sister of Sir George Mackenzie of Tarbat, the famous lawyer, the lady being at the time of the marriage, about thirty years of age. There were born to them a son, named Hugh, who, from a black spot on his upper lip, was nick-named " Mac-Shimi, Ball Dubh," " Black-spotted Mackimmie ; " and three daughters.

XVI. Hugh, " The Black-spotted," succeeded as twelfth Lord Lovat. He married a daughter of Murray, Marquis of Athole, a connection in which the pretensions of the Murrays, thwarted by Simon of Beaufort, find their source. This chief left four daughters, but no son, and having had no brothers or uncles on the father's side, the succession went to Thomas of Beaufort, surviving son of Hugh, the tenth Lord Lovat, and grand-uncle of Hugh, " The Black-spotted."

XVII. Thomas of Beaufort assumed the title as thirteenth Lord Lovat, and would probably have been left in undisputed possession but for the marriage contract made by the twelfth Lord, at the instance of the Athols, settling the estates on his eldest daughter, failing male heirs of his body. It is true that afterwards he revoked this settlement in favor of the nearest male heir, viz., Thomas of Beaufort, but the validity of the later document was contested, and it was only after a long and extraordinary struggle, in which plot, intrigue and violence played a part, as well as protracted litigation, that his son's title to the estates was confirmed.

XVIII. SIMON of Beaufort succeeded his father, as fourteenth Lord Lovat, after, as has been stated, many years of fierce contest concerning his rights. He had an elder brother, named Alexander, who, according to report then current, died young in Wales, and without issue. His younger brothers were named Hugh, John, Thomas, and James. The cause of Alexander's flight to Wales forms one of the best known legends of the family. There are various versions of it, but I shall give that most commonly related by old people in the district of the Aird: Alexander arrived, somewhat late, at a wedding at Teawig, near Beauly. His appearance was the signal for the piper to strike up the tune, "Tha Biodag air MacThomais," some of the lines of which run:

> Tha biodag air Mac Thomais,
> Tha biodag fhada, mhor, air;
> Tha biodag air Mac Thomais,
> Ach's math a dh' fhoghnadh sgian da.
>
> Tha biodag anns a chliobadaich,
> Air mac a bhodaich leibidich;
> Tha biodag anns a chliobadaich,
> Air mac a bhodaich romaich.
>
> Tha bhiodag deanadh gliogadaich,
> 'Si ceann'lt ri bann na briogais aig';
> Tha bucallan 'n a bhrogan,
> Ged 's math a dh' fhoghnadh ial daibh.

It was whispered to Alexander that the piper selected this tune to cause merriment at his expense, and the youth, to turn the jest against the piper, determined to rip open the bag of the pipes, with his dirk. But in doing so, his foot slipped, and he fell heavily towards the piper with the naked dirk in his outstretched arm. The piper was fatally wounded, and Alexander, who had been an extreme partizan of the Jacobites, believed that were he tried for the murder of the piper, the hostility of Sir George Mackenzie, of Tarbat, would inevitably secure a sentence of death against him. He fled to Wales, where he was befriended by Earl Powis, under whose protection, it is said, he lived on, married, and had issue, while his next younger brother, Simon, enjoyed the title and estates. Mr. John Fraser, of Mount Pleasant, Carnarvon, not long ago, laid claim to the chiefship, title and estates, on the ground that he is a lineal descendant of this Alexander, and although he lost his case in one trial, he is still gathering evidence, with the view of having it re-opened and further pushing his claim.

For his share in the Jacobite rising of 1745, Simon, fourteenth Lord Lovat, was beheaded on Tower Hill, April 9th, 1747. Lord Simon's faults were not few, but he has been a much maligned man ; his vices have been flaunted before the world, his virtues have been obscured. In extreme old age he gave up his life on the scaffold ; and his fate, believed by some to be richly deserved, by others has been characterized as martyrdom. He left three sons, Simon, Alexander and Archibald Campbell Fraser.

XIX. SIMON succeeded to the chiefship, but that honor was unaccompanied by the estates and title, which had been forfeited to the crown. For his services as commandant of Fraser's Highlanders in the service of the House of Hanover, he was specially thanked by Parliament, and the paternal estates restored to him. I have been informed by the Grand Master Mason of Ontario that this Colonel Simon (afterwards General Simon Fraser of Lovat) was the first Provincial Master Mason in Upper Canada, the order having been established there at the time of the stirring events in which Fraser's Highlanders participated while in Quebec. General Simon married, but without issue, and his brother Alexander having predeceased him without issue, he was succeeded in possession of the estates by his half-brother,

XX. COLONEL ARCHIBALD CAMPBELL FRASER of Lovat. The title was still held in abeyance. Colonel Archibald was a man of erratic habits, but a kind-hearted Highlander, and a man of no mean ability. An account of his honors and public services he embodied in an inscription on his tombstone, but while the production is typical of his well-known eccentricity, as a matter of fact, not a little of the praise which he takes to himself for services to his country and his county, was well deserved. He had five sons, all of whom predeceased him. His eldest son was named Simon Frederick. He became member of Parliament for Inverness-shire. He died in 1803, unmarried, but left one son, Archibald Thomas Frederick Fraser, well-known in our own day as "Abertarf," from having resided there. None of the other sons of Colonel Archibald left legitimate issue, and at his death, in 1815, the succession reverted to the Frasers of Strichen, descended, as already observed, from Thomas Fraser of Knockie and Strichen. second son of Alexander, the sixth Lord Lovat, represented, at the time of Colonel Archibald's death, by

XXI. THOMAS ALEXANDER FRASER, of Strichen, who succeeded to the estates, and was created Lord Lovat by Act of Parliament, in 1837; and, in 1857, succeeded in having the old title restored to him. The succession of the Strichen family created a strong hostile feeling among the Clansmen and the old tenants generally, many of them believing that other aspirants who appeared had stronger claims. The Frasers of Strichen, however, were able to satisfy the courts as to the validity of their claim, and they were confirmed in the possession of the estates. A curious incident of the time may be briefly related, to illustrate both the feeling then prevailing concerning the succession, and the religious beliefs which were held then in the Highlands. It was, and to some extent yet is, believed that the Divine purpose, with respect to every-day events, may be disclosed in appropriate portions of Scripture which impress themselves intensely on the mind of the devout believer. Two tenant-farmers, whose names, if given, would at once be a guarantee of their good faith, and of their respectability, went from the vicinity of Belladrum to the neighborhood of Redcastle, to a man whose piety gave him an eminent place among The Men of Ross-shire. They went to confer with him about the Lovat estates, and to find out whether he had any "indication" of the "mind of the Lord" as to whether the Frasers of Strichen would be established in their tenure of the estates against all comers. They were hospitably welcomed, and, their errand having been made known, their host replied that he had had no such indication. They remained that night, the next day and the night following, but during all this time did not see their host. On the morning of the third day he joined them at the frugal breakfast, after which he led them to a window overlooking the Beauly Firth and said: "Since your arrival I have pled hard for light at the Throne. If God ever did reveal His Will to me by His Word, He did so last night. You see a fishing-smack before you on the firth; as sure as you do observe her there, with her sail spread, catching the wind, so sure will, in God's good time, the Strichens pass away from the possession of the Lovat estates, and the rightful heir will come to his own. My warrant, given to me in my wrestling with God, is this prophetic passage: 'And thou, profane, wicked prince of Israel, whose day is come, when iniquity shall have an end, thus saith the Lord God: Remove the diadem, and take off the crown: this shall not be the same: exalt him that is low, and abase him that is high. I will overturn, overturn, overturn it : and it shall be no more, until he come whose right it is ; and I will give it him.' (Ezek. XXI., 25-27) God's purpose thus revealed will not be fulfilled in our day, nor likely in the day of our children, but our grandchildren will likely see it accomplished." The old man's words made a deep impression ; but only a few friends were informed of them, not only because they were held as a sacred message, but also because of the " power of the estate office." Whatever may be thought of beliefs thus formed, no one who knew the devout, simple-hearted Highlander of the generation just gone, will fail to appreciate the humility and sincerity with which such beliefs were entertained.

But to return to the fortunes of the House of Lovat. Thomas Alexander, fifteenth Lord Lovat, married a daughter of Sir George Jerningham, afterwards Baron Stafford, and had male issue, Simon, Allister Edward, George Edward Stafford (b. 1834, d. 1854), and Henry Thomas. His second son, Allister Edward, rose to the rank of Colonel in the army ; was married, with issue, one son. Hon. Henry Thomas attained to the rank of Colonel of the 1st battalion Scots Guards. Lord Lovat died in 1885, and was succeeded by his eldest son,

XXII. SIMON, sixteenth Lord Lovat, who, born in 1828, and married to the daughter of Thomas Weld Blundell, was already a man of mature years at the time of his accession. He was known in song as " Fear Donn an Fheilidh." He was noted for his generous qualities and his kindness to the poor. He was a keen sportsman, expert with rod, gun and rifle, a marksman of repute. He did much to encourage the militia movement, and commanded the Inverness-shire regiment for many years. The circumstances of his sad and sudden death, from an affection of the heart, while grouse-shooting on the Moy Hall moors, in 1887, are fresh in our minds. An extract from a newspaper article, written on the occasion of his death, may be taken as a fair estimate of his character: " By this sudden and painful blow a nobleman has been taken away who filled a conspicuous place in this vicinity, and who was held in the highest respect. Having succeeded to his father in 1875, he has enjoyed the title and estates for only twelve years (1887). But as Master of Lovat he was known for many years before that time as a worthy and popular representative of a great and ancient Highland house. No county gathering seemed to be complete without his presence. . . . Homely in his manner, he was never difficult to approach, and his kindness of spirit showed itself in many ways. Conscientious and sober in judgment, he steadily endeavored to do his duty; and his lamented death caused a blank which cannot easily be filled." He left a family of nine, and was succeeded by his eldest son,

XXIII. SIMON JOSEPH, seventeenth Lord Lovat, to whose health, as our chief, we have drained our glasses this evening. That he may have a long and happy life is our fervent prayer; and may God grant him wisdom and grace that he may be a useful and a prosperous chief; that he may add new lustre to the distinguished name he bears, and prove worthy of the ancestry of which he is the proud representative.

We have now traced the long line of chiefs from the beginning down to the present day, and I must thank you for the wonderful patience with which you have listened to the dry bones of genealogy; in what remains* I hope I shall prove less tedious than in that which I have concluded.

*This part of the speech, being of a general character, has been omitted for consideration of space.

The speaker then referred briefly to the Aberdeenshire Frasers, and to some of the principal Cadet families of the Clan. He gave an explanation of the coat of arms, related a number of interesting Clan incidents, including forays, Clan feuds, and anecdotes of a local character. At some length he described the Home of the Clan, pointing out its extent on a map of Inverness-shire, colored to show the gradual increase and decrease of territory, which kept pace with the varying fortunes of the Clan; expatiating on the great variety and beauty of its scenery, tributes to which he quoted from Christopher North, David Macrae, Robert Carruthers and Evan MacColl.

Mr. Robert Lovat Fraser, Vice-chairman, replied to the toast. He said: My duty, through the kindness of the committee, is certainly not so arduous in replying to the toast of the evening, as that which has been imposed upon the Chairman in proposing it. The length of his address, the facts regarding the origin and the outlines of the history of the Clan which he gave, make it unnecessary for me to dwell at length on this interesting topic. Indeed, I found on listening to the Chairman, that I had a great deal to learn about our Clan, and I am sure that I express not only my own thanks, but yours to him, in placing before us, so clearly and minutely, the leading facts regarding our ancestry and kindred. All my life long I have been an ardent admirer of some of the more prominent Frasers who have figured in our Clan history. My own connection with the Clan in the Highlands is somewhat remote, the last of my forefathers who resided there having had to leave his home and friends, on account of the part which he took with his Clan in the uprising of '45. But although we have been cut off from that close connection which is thought necessary to keep alive a sentimental interest in such things, I can assure you that no clansman born within the shadow of Castle Downie can boast with greater truth of possessing more enthusiasm and interest than I in all that pertains to the Clan Fraser. The Clan has a history which we as clansmen should so study as to become perfectly familiar with it. Its record has been written in the events of the times as well as on the page of history, and no more inspiring or patriotic duty lies to our hand than the study of that record. I firmly believe that the influence of the clan feeling was a good influence, and that the idea of kinship and responsibility to each other for good behavior, as

MR. ROBERT LOVAT FRASER,
1st Vice-Chairman.

to kinsmen, had much to do in bringing about the high moral tone which distinguishes the Highland clans. It did much also to prepare the minds of those people for the enlightenment and love which Christianity brought with it, and which are so strikingly exemplified in the Highland character. I would say therefore to the young men, 'employ part of your evenings in the reading of the Clan history,' and to the older people, 'devote a little of the time of your remaining years to a like purpose.' I do not think it necessary, after what we have just heard, to enter into historic details; neither is it necessary to defend the honor of the Clan where there are no assailants. The Clan has taken its place honorably among its contemporaries and neighbors. It invariably performed its duty in a manner highly creditable to the public spirit of its members and to their high standard of justice. There were it is true at times in the Clan, as in every other body of people, men whose names have been perpetuated because of evil rather than good. These, however, have been singularly few in the Clan Fraser, and even where statements are found to their discredit, the malice of interested foes not infrequently lends a heightened color to charges which might to some extent have been founded on fact. This I believe to be true in the case of Simon Lord Lovat, who had the misfortune to be the subject of biographical sketches by his enemies, but of whom a juster view now prevails. Happily the prominent clansmen, whose characteristics needed no defence, but called forth admiration and emulation, were many. To name them would be but to recite a long and distinguished list. Their characteristics were such as to challenge public commendation. With them as examples no clansman need feel ashamed of the name. But what I should like to impress most of all upon our Clan throughout the country is the necessity for a sentiment of loyalty to the Clan name and its traditions. Seeing that we have such a history let us prize it. Let every clansman feel proud of it, and let him see to it that his conduct and ambition are in every way in keeping with the record of the past, and in this way prove himself not only a good citizen, a good neighbor and a good friend, but a good clansman, and hand down the character of the Clan unsullied to posterity. This would be a most laudable ambition and one which I feel sure every Fraser worthy of the name will strive earnestly to attain.

Two gentlemen, Frasers all but in name, had been invited as guests. They were Mr. B. Homer Dixon, Consul General for the Netherlands, and Mr. Hugh Miller, J. P., both of Toronto. Their health was proposed by the chairman, who paid a high compliment to Mr. Homer Dixon, who, he said, had taken the warmest interest in matters relating to the Clan, and who was a living encyclopedia of information regarding its history and affairs. Mr. Dixon's connection was derived from his maternal side, and not a few Clan relics were in his possession. His absence from the gathering was on account of indifferent health, and it was regretted very much by those present. In coupling Mr. Miller's name with the toast, the Chairman referred to that gentleman's long connection with the business interests of the city of Toronto. Mr. Hugh Miller was a relative of his namesake, the famous geologist, and his name was as well known in Ontario business and national circles, as was that of his distinguished namesake in the field of literature and science. Mr. Miller rightly claimed to be of Fraser stock—he certainly had the Fraser spirit. He sat with them as an honored guest, but none the less an honored clansman.

Mr. Miller, in reply, expressed the great satisfaction with which he had received an invitation to be present at what he might truly describe as a gathering of his own clansmen. It was well known that in Scotland, as in other countries, men were often named after the occupations which they followed, and it was not a mere tradition but a fact within the knowledge of his immediate forebears that they were of pure Fraser stock. They had worn the Fraser tartan, and had always taken a deep interest in whatever pertained to the affairs of the Clan. When the Chairman, in giving the toast of the Clan, had referred to the places associated with the name, he was brought back in memory over a long period of time. At his age, the sweep of memory to boyhood's days was a long one, and he could well recall the events in the Highlands of Scotland over sixty years ago. He had a loving and familiar recollection of scenes, than which there were none more beautiful under the sun, and of people who had animated these fair surroundings. The Fraser estates were among the finest in Britain, affording examples of beauty calculated to leave a very vivid impression on the youthful mind, and during his long life his early impressions had ever remained fresh and green. He remembered the time when the succession to the chiefship and estates was in hot dispute, and he knew how deeply the clansmen were moved by that contest. Down to that day the feeling of the clans was as strong as of old, and doubtless if occasion arose, it would prove to be strong still. At that time there were various claimants for the honors and possessions of the ancient house of Lovat, and as a boy he saw a good deal of those who were prominently concerned in the case. The Frasers were very anxious that the true heir by blood should succeed, and much was privately as well as openly done on behalf of the various contestants, according as the clansmen believed in the various claims put forward. As to the main object of their re-union that evening, he could do nothing but express his sincere hope that a strong association of the Frasers would be formed. There was no reason whatever why such an organization should not flourish in Canada, where those bearing the name could be numbered by thousands.

He had the good fortune to know not a few Frasers in Canada, and he could honestly say that none of them, so far as he knew, ever did anything that in any way tarnished the good name of the Clan. He had great hopes of the success of the movement from the enthusiasm of the gathering, and from the fact that those who had taken the matter in hand were men of energy and capacity. He could now only thank them for having honored the toast in such a hospitable manner, and wish them all success in the projected organization.

"The Clan in Canada."

Mr. R. Lovat Fraser, Vice-chairman, in proposing the toast of "The Clan in Canada," said: The Clan in Canada is not, of course, as important as the Clan at large, but it has an importance altogether its own, and has a record not unworthy the parent stem. It is a branch of a goodly tree, and bears fruit of the finest quality. No clan has done more, if as much, for Canada as the Clan Fraser. Coming with the famous Seventy-Eighth regiment they did their duty at Louisburg and Quebec, and stamped the Clan name indelibly on the history of Canada, from ocean to ocean. Not only did they render services in the east, but in pioneer work helped to open up the west by travel, trade and commerce. A distinguished clansman and a relation of my friend on the right (Fraserfield) was the discoverer of the Fraser River. To those of us who highly prize the integrity of the British Empire it must be a source of pride to know that the part taken by the Seventy-Eighth in Lower Canada helped very much to keep the American continent for the British Crown. The history of that time clearly proves that had the fortunes of war been adverse in Canada to the British arms, the French would have been in a position to overrun and seize the whole of North America. This is a fact which is sometimes lost sight of, but is one of much satisfaction to us as clansmen. To those whose names have been coupled with this interesting toast, I must leave the duty of dealing at length with it, and I rejoice that both of them are gentlemen thoroughly familiar with the subject and of recognized ability as speakers. I refer to Mr. E. A. Fraser, barrister. of Detroit, and our worthy friend, Mr. G. B. Fraser, of Toronto.

Mr. E. A. Fraser said : Mr. Vice-chairman, Chairman and Clansmen, although hailing from the other side of the line, I am a Canadian-born clansman, my native place being Bowmanville, near this beautiful Queen City. I passed my younger days in this province, attended the schools here, and am as familiar with the affairs of the country and with our clansmen in the country as those who have not left it to reside under another flag. I can therefore speak with confidence to this toast, but you will excuse me if I speak briefly, as the honor was unexpected, and I do not wish to make it appear that any words of mine that may come on the spur of the moment would be sufficient to lay before you, in proper form, what our Clan has done for Canada and the position which it occupies to-day in the affairs of the country. It is easy to speak of Louisburg and Quebec ; it is easy to dilate on the names of distinguished clansmen familiar to us all for the prominent positions they have taken among their fellows, but the work performed by the Clan in Canada would not then be half told. We must go back to the hoary forests, to the backwoods, where the early settlers bent their energies to the opening up of the country. That noble pioneer work in which our clansmen shared, and shared in large numbers, it seems to me, has an importance that is not as often recognized as it ought to be. It is difficult for the imagination even to grasp the peculiar task that lay before the early settlers of this vast, heavily-timbered, unbroken, unopened, untravelled country. Now that we can take a seat in the railway car at Halifax and leave it at Vancouver, we can form but the very faintest conception of what this country was one hundred years ago, when those hardy mountaineers ranged themselves alongside the Lowland Scot, the Englishman, the Irishman, the German and the Frenchman, to hew down the lords of the forest, to turn the wilderness into well cultivated fields, to turn the log cabins into the mansions that now adorn the plains, and to form, as they do, a sturdy peasantry second to none in the world. When the pen of a genius has dealt with those times, a chapter will be written for the civilized world more interesting, probably, than any yet penned. We have to leave the high places of military fame and statesmanship and enter the factory and the counting-house to trace there the career of the pioneers of industry and commerce, and among them we find our clansmen performing those duties which the necessities of the country demanded. If we turn to the professions, our Clan is found to hold its own. To the church, to law, to medicine, to art, to politics, we have given men of whom we are proud. The walk of life in Canada that has not been trodden by a clansman would be only an undesirable one for any man to tread. If I may be permitted to say it—coming as I do from the great State of Michigan—I would say that in that State, where our clansmen are very numerous, they not only hold their own, but have attained to eminence in business and in the professions. We have men of distinguished ability at the head of the legal fraternity of our State ; we have men whose genius in business has secured them wealth and position ; we have men who in humbler spheres have rendered patriotic services to the State, and who, one and all, show that they have not lost the characteristics of the Clan in new associations and callings. Before sitting down I should like to express the great pleasure I have experienced at this gathering of clansmen. I would have come twice as far to be present, and trust that the organization, the formation of which will undoubtedly be sanctioned here to-night, will be the means of bringing us together frequently to enjoy ourselves as we are now doing.

Mr. G. B. Fraser, of Toronto, followed, in response to the same toast. He said : Mr. Vice-chairman, Chairman and Clansmen, I frequently have to regret my lack of ability to discharge a duty of this nature to my own satisfaction The subject allotted to me is one with which I cannot claim to be unfamiliar. It is a subject of great interest, and on such an occasion as the present, a subject which ought to be treated with some detail in order to perpetuate the names and deeds of clansmen who have done their duty nobly and well by this the land of our adoption. I find myself, however, not lacking in material, but in that ability--which seems to be born in some men—to place my information lucidly and briefly before you. Some speakers have already referred, and others will, later on, refer to the origin of the Clan Fraser in Canada. I shall not trespass on that part of the subject, but coming down to this century we find a clansman whose name will ever live in Canada. I refer to Simon Fraser, the discoverer of the Fraser River, whose life, when it comes to be written, will certainly shed lustre on the Clan name. He was descended from a cadet family of the

A MILITARY PROJECT. 71

Lovats, came with his mother (Vermont) ~~parents~~ to Canada from the Eastern States, and settled at Glengarry. His worthy relative, Fraser of Fraserfield, sits here on my right, and proud I am to welcome him to this feast. John Fraser de Berry, the founder of the New Clan Fraser, was a man of extraordinary personality, whose acquaintance I first made at the time of the Trent affair. I happened to be in Montreal at that time, and received a telegram from De Berry that he wished to see me. He came from Quebec city, and we met in the St. Lawrence Hall. I was very much impressed with the singular interview which took place between us. Of course he was full of the project of his Clan Fraser, full of the history and genealogy of the Clan. He was an enthusiast, and in common with many enthusiasts could look but with impatience on the practical, prosaic side of things. With due formality, acting by what he believed to be his authority as a chieftain of the Clan, he invested me with power to raise a company of Frasers, in an allotted district in Western Ontario, which was delineated on a military plan in his possession. I could not do otherwise than accept the commission, which was that of captain, from this venerable-looking and earnest chief. Had I been able to withdraw from business, I have no doubt that I should have been, in a very short time, at the head of a company numbering at least one hundred stalwart clansmen, who would have given a good account of themselves in the field. But, as you are aware, the occasion for defence quickly passed away, and no more was heard of the proposed regiment of Frasers, of which my company was to have formed a part. The most remarkable fact which impressed itself upon me then, and one that I yet consider remarkable, was the manner in which De Berry had the Province divided into military districts on his maps, the exact information which he had regarding the locations in which the clansmen resided, and the mass of details with which he seemed to be perfectly familiar. I could not understand how he acquired all this information, but have been informed since, by some who were associated with him, that he spared no means to trace out every Fraser in the country, through the voters' lists, the township registration books and the village directories. The amount of work involved in such research must have been enormous, and I can well believe that for many years De Berry devoted his time, as a man of leisure, to this project. He also appointed me as one of the one hundred and eleven chieftains of the New Clan, the chief of which was a descendant of a cadet of the Lovat family, residing in Nova Scotia, but the organization was too unwieldy, and its objects were rather vague for practical purposes. For a number of years meetings were held in Montreal of a very interesting character, but with De Berry's death and that of a number of those more prominently associated with him interest died out, and now we hear of the New Clan no more. We can profit by their experience in our own undertaking, and doubtless we shall be able to form an organization which will live, and which will perpetuate the name and traditions associated with the name and with this new country. I have practically confined myself to De Berry's name, not because there is a lack of clansmen on my list, whose memories deserve to be perpetuated, such as, for instance, the founder of the Fraser Institute, in Montreal ; John Fraser, the author ; John A. Fraser, the artist; Judge Fraser and Colonel Fraser, of Glengarry ; but because some of these will doubtless be alluded to by other speakers, and, because having devoted so much time to a man whose name and personality I cannot but regard as of peculiar interest to us, I have left myself but little time to refer to those clansmen whom I held, and still hold, in high esteem, and in whose name I thank you for the toast proposed and honored in such a fitting manner.

"Distinguished Clansmen."

Mr. R. L. Fraser, the Vice-chairman, then proposed the toast of " Distinguished Clansmen in Art, Science, Literature, Theology, Arms and Politics." He said : I had almost concluded that all Frasers are distinguished clansmen, and distinguished in the highest sense of the word, though it were better, perhaps, to be more modest, and hence the division into which this toast has been divided. While we rightly draw much of our inspiration from the seat of the Clan across the sea, it is well that we should remember, and remember generously, those of our Clan in this country who have secured high positions in life. Among our artists the name " Fraser " takes high rank. Some of the Fraser artists I have known personally, and can bear testimony not only to their fame, but to their personal qualities. Canadian art owes much to Mr. J. A. Fraser and Mr. W. Lewis Fraser, now sojourning in Europe. Literature claims the names of James Lovat Fraser, the distinguished classical scholar, of John Fraser, of Donald Fraser, and others well known in Canada. Science also has its devotees and distinguished students, especially medical science and theology. Frasers both in Canada and in the old land have taken front rank in the profession of arms, and have distinguished themselves from the time of Sir Simon Fraser, the compeer and companion of Wallace and the savior of Scotland, down to the present day. In politics the

Clan has certainly won its share of such honors as the public delight to bestow. The reply to this toast has been entrusted to a splendid array of able clansmen. For clansmen distinguished in arts, Ex-Mayor Fraser, of Petrolea, will reply; for those in science, Dr. J. B. Fraser; for those in theology, Dr. Mungo Fraser; for those in literature, Professor W. H. Fraser; for Frasers in war, Mr. Alexander Fraser (Fraserfield); and for those in politics, Mr. W. P. Fraser.

Ex-Mayor Fraser, replying for the "Frasers in Art," said: Mr. Chairman and Gentlemen,—Your committee, in selecting me to speak for our clansmen in Art, acted of course on the assumption that I possessed the necessary qualifications for the task. At the outset, however, I must, in justice to all concerned, but more especially to the Frasers who have won distinction in art, confess that my attainments in that department are hardly such as to entitle me to a hearing in response to this important toast. But I am to some extent emboldened and sustained by the reflection that, as this is in a sense a family gathering, the shortcomings of a Fraser will pass, if not unobserved, at least without provoking unfriendly comment. Permit me then, on behalf of the artists of our Clan, to thank you for the cordial and enthusiastic manner in which you have received this toast. Among the many distinguished clansmen who have, in almost every sphere of human endeavor and usefulness, shed unfading lustre, not only upon our Clan, but upon humanity in general, our artists have secured an honored place. Of necessity, those of our Clan who have excelled in art are few in number; indeed, the artists of the world and of the ages might almost find standing room in this banquet hall. But our Clan has perhaps produced its quota, and some of them have taken high rank. It is not my purpose to mention the names of all; in fact, I am unable to name more than two, viz., Charles Fraser and John A. Fraser. The former was a distinguished portrait painter of South Carolina who died in 1860 at the age of 78 years. He left a large number of portraits, all of which are said to have much artistic merit, and some of which have acquired considerable historic value. Of Mr. John A. Fraser it is hardly necessary to speak here. By his works we know him. A collection of Canadian paintings without one or more of his masterly representations of Canadian scenery would assuredly be incomplete. Let that suffice for our modern artists. It occurs to me, as it must have done to us all at one time or another, that our Clan must have produced great artists in the bygone ages. Assuredly Greece and Italy did not produce *all* the old masters. The Fraser Clan flourished then and was of course represented in art; but, just as in the newspaper—the product of the "art preservative"—there is to be found an occasional artist who, impelled by modesty or an exaggerated regard for his personal

Ex-Mayor John Fraser,
2nd Vice-Chairman.

safety, uses a *nom de plume*—for instance, "Junius," *Vox Populi* or "A Disgusted Subscriber"—so there were, I fancy, in the days of long ago, Frasers in art who unmindful of posterity or perchance distrustful of their own powers, as genius so frequently is, worked under cover of such names as Raphael, Leonardo da Vinci, Michael Angelo, Canova, etc. A slight effort of the imagination will enable a Fraser to accept this theory.

The Fraser has ever been great on the "tented field." There, indeed, he has won renown, for his "fierce, native daring" has never been surpassed. But there are still victories to be won, infinitely greater than any achieved in battle. The grandest painting is yet to be painted, and we who are the first in Canada to assemble in honor of our ancient and beloved Clan shall ever fondly cherish the hope that the first place in art will be occupied by a Fraser. But from whatever clan or country the master shall come, the Frasers will be among the first to do him honor.

I thank you, Mr. Chairman and gentlemen, for the patient hearing you have given me.

The reply to the part of this toast referring to "Science" was made by Dr. J. B. Fraser, M. D., C. M., R. C. P. and S. K., Toronto. He said: Mr. Chairman, Vice-chairman, and Brother Clansmen, it gives me a great deal of pleasure to meet such a representative gathering of the old and distinguished "Clan Fraser" as we have here to-night. It arouses one's enthusiasm to think of the leading position our forefathers took in the history of Scotland, and the many deeds of valor performed on the battle field; and although they were pre-eminently noted as warriors, still we have many instances in which they shone in the realms of science. In replying to the toast of "The Frasers in Science," allow me to give you a few brief biographical sketches of a few of our ancestors.

Sir Alexander Fraser, of Philorth, was born in 1537, and died in 1623. He succeeded his grandfather to the estates in 1569, and at once began to improve the estate and advance the welfare of his clansmen. At this time Philorth was the baronial burgh, and boasted of a commodious harbor; but after the improvements referred to he changed the name to Fraserburgh. Having conceived the idea of founding a university, in spite of the strenuous opposition of the town of Aberdeen, he obtained powers to build a university at Fraserburgh, with all the privileges of the older universities. The remains of this building still existed in 1888. On account of his interest in education and high scholastic attainments he was knighted in 1594. His motto was "The glory of the honorable is to fear God."

John Fraser, F. L. S., was born in 1750, and died in 1811. He was a noted botanist, and visited North America five times in search of new and unknown specimens. He collected a great many plants in Newfoundland and later on at Charleston, Virginia. In 1796 he visited St. Petersburg, where he was introduced to the notice of the Empress Catherine, who purchased his entire collection of plants. In 1798 he was appointed botanical collector to the Czar Paul, and by him sent to America for a fresh collection. As a tribute to his ability he was elected a Fellow of Linnean Society (F.L.S.)

Sir Alexander Fraser, M. D., belonged to the Durris branch of the family. He was educated at Aberdeen University, and having risen by his skill high in the ranks of physicians and surgeons he was appointed physician to Charles II., whom he accompanied in his travels through Scotland. Spotswood, in his history of Scotland, speaks highly of his learning and skill. He died in 1681.

Robt. Fraser, F. R. S., son of Rev. Geo. Fraser, was born in 1760, and educated in Glasgow University, where he obtained the degree of M.A., when he was but 15 years of age. He studied for the Church of Scotland, and was appointed in an official capacity to the Prince of Wales, afterward George IV. In 1791 the Earl of Breadalbane asked him to accompany him on a tour through the Western Isles and the Highlands of Scotland, undertaken with the view of improving the state of the people. The Prince of Wales gave him leave, and at the same time stated his faith in his ability to plan some means by which the people would be benefited, and wished him success. He succeeded so well that he was chosen to conduct a statistical survey of Ireland, and was the means of originating several important works, among others the harbor of Kingstown, sometimes called Queenstown. He published several works on agriculture, mines, mineralogy, fish, etc. He died in 1831.

Simon Fraser was an explorer of some note, and was sent by the Hudson's Bay Company to establish new trading posts, and prospect for minerals, etc. He wrote many papers from 1806 to 1808. The Fraser river was named after him.*

Lewis Fraser was a zoologist of some note, and was appointed as curator of the Zoological Society of London. He travelled through South America, studying the character and habits of different animals and birds, and as the result of his travels published a work called " Zoologia Typica," or

* See sketch of his life later on.

figures of rare and new animals. In 1888 his son was curator of the Zoological and General Sections of the Indian Museum of Calcutta.

William Fraser, LL. D., was born in 1817 in Banffshire, and was ordained pastor of the Free Middle congregation of Paisley in 1849. In 1872 the University of Glasgow conferred on him the degree of LL. D., on account of his scientific attainments. In 1873, in recognition of his long services as President of the Philosophical Society, he was presented with a microscope and purse of sovereigns. He died in 1879.

Alexander Campbell Fraser, D. C. L., LL. D., was born in 1819. His father was a minister and his mother a sister of Sir Duncan Campbell. He was educated in

MR. WILLIAM A. FRASER,
SECRETARY-TREASURER.

the Universities of Edinburgh and Glasgow, and in 1842 won a prize for his essay on "Toleration." In 1859 he was Dean of the Faculty in Arts, University of Edinburgh, and in 1871 was appointed Examiner in Moral Science; the same year he received the degree of LL.D. from the University of Glasgow. Later he was appointed Examiner in Moral Science and Logic at the India Civil Service Examinations. He was elected a member of the Athenian Club—without a ballot—for eminence in literature and philosophy. He afterward received the Degree of D. C. L., Oxford University.

Professor Thos. Richard Fraser, M. D., F. R. S., was born in Calcutta, India, in 1841, and graduated in medicine in Edinburgh in 1862. In 1863 he acted as Assistant Professor of Materia Medica, and in 1869 was appointed as Assistant Physician in the Royal Infirmary. He was afterward appointed Examiner in Materia Medica in London University, and was elected Medical Health Officer for Mid-Cheshire; he was also appointed Examiner in Public Health by London University. He was Dean of the Faculty in 1880 He is a F. R. S., F. R. C. P., Edinburgh; member of the Pharmaceutical Society, Britain; corresponding member of the Therapeutical Society of Paris, and of the Academy of Natural Sciences of Philadelphia. When the International Medical Congress met in London in 1881 he was appointed president of one section, and again president of one section in 1885. His work has been chiefly in the direction of determining the physiological effects of medicinal substances, with the view of establishing an accurate and rational basis for the treatment of disease.

I have now mentioned some of the names recorded in history of Frasers that were distinguished in Science, and as I have occupied more than my share of time, I will take my seat, conscious that I have been able to mention but a few of the many clansmen distinguished for their scientific attainments. As I said at the outset I have enjoyed a great deal of pleasure in this gathering of clansmen. In looking over the record of a few of our brethren distinguished in science, so as to glean a few facts for this occasion, I recognized more than ever before the substantial services rendered to mankind by men bearing our name, and now that we have foregathered a small company, it may be, but a select one, I feel that you share with me the pride with which we regard our Clan and name.

Professor W. H. Fraser, in replying to the sentiment, " Distinguished Clansmen in Literature," said : Gentlemen, —I thank you heartily for the way in which you have received this toast, and for the honor you confer on me in asking me to answer for our distinguished literary clansmen living and dead.

Literature is the mirror of life. Life is action : literature is contemplation and words. My knowledge of the history of the Clan leads me to the conclusion that most of its distinguished members were men of deeds rather than words, and that they lived at times and under circumstances when deeds rather than words had value—men like Sir Alexander, who fought by Robert Bruce's side at Bannockburn, or that other Sir Alexander Mackenzie Fraser of the last century, described by contemporaries as "mild as a lamb and strong as a lion," who had said to him in public by his General, "Colonel Fraser, you and your regiment have this day saved the British army," or the Fraser who fought with Wolfe before Quebec, and a host of others· These men did not write literature, but perhaps they were better employed. I think they were, but at any rate they are the men who furnish the basis for literature—heroism, fidelity and devotion.

The Clan has, however, not been wanting in scholars and

writers, nor in those who patronized and furthered learning. What think you of a Fraser—Sir Alexander of Philorth—who in the 16th century built a grand University? It is getting to be the fashion now for rich men to build and endow seats of learning, but a man with such foresight and generosity in those early times in Scotland is surely deserving of all praise.

Although not a few of the early Frasers won fame by the sword, some wielded to good purpose that mightier weapon, the pen. Such was James Fraser of Brea, in Ross-shire, who wrote copiously on theology, and who went to prison, by orders of Archbishop Sharp, as a preacher at conventicles. Another divine and scholar was James Fraser, of Pitcalzian, in Ross-shire, a son of the manse; a famous controversialist he was, and wrote a book against the Arminianism of Grotius that has kept its ground in Scotland till the present day, although he died as long ago as 1769.

These are some of our older literary celebrities. Time will not permit me to mention all those who belong to the present century, or whose lives extended into it. There was Archibald Campbell Fraser of Lovat, 38th McShimi, who died in 1815. As a school-boy he saw the fight at Culloden, and was afterwards Foreign Consul in Barbary, and was author of the "Annals of the patriots of the family of Fraser, Frizell, Simson or Fitzsimson." It must in truth have been a mighty book if it recorded them all. A curious piece of literature from his pen was the very long and very laudatory epitaph for his own tomb erected by himself.

Robert Fraser, of Pathhead, Fifeshire, lived up till 1839. He was an ironmonger, but of such remarkable literary and linguistic tastes that in leisure moments he acquired Latin,

Greek, French, German, Italian and Spanish. His poetry, which I regret is not accessible to me, was, it is said, characterized by fine feeling and nicety of touch. Truly a remarkable man. His ruling passion was strong in death, for he passed out of life dictating some translations of Norwegian and Danish poems.

There are other ways of making literature besides writing it yourself. James Fraser, an Inverness man, was one of those who have made literature by proxy. Who does not know Fraser's Magazine? that pioneer publication in this field of literature, dating from 1830, with its famous contributors like Thackeray, Carlyle, J. A. Froude and Father Prout. This Fraser was also a famous publisher, a man of taste and judgment, and did more to advance literature than almost any man of his time, notwithstanding Carlyle's reference to him as " that infatuated Fraser with his dog's-meat tart of a magazine."

Contemporary with Fraser of the magazine was James Baillie Fraser, also an Inverness man and a famous traveller who explored the Himalaya Mountains, and who was the first European to reach the sources of the Jumna and Ganges. He came home, and wrote an account of his travels. A little later he donned Persian costume, explored the larger part of Persia, and wrote a two-volume account of his journey. Turning to romance, he wrote " Kuggilbas," a tale of Khorasain; and this was the first of a long list of Eastern tales, histories and travels, the mere enumeration of which would take us on pretty far towards to-morrow morning.

A beautiful and sympathetic literary figure is that of Lydia Falconer Fraser, the wife of Hugh Miller. Here are some lines from a poem of hers on the death of their first-born child :

> "Thou'rt awa, awa, from thy mother's side,
> And awa, awa, from thy father's knee;
> Thou'rt awa from our blessing, our care, our caressing,
> But awa from our hearts thou'lt never be.
>
> * * * * *
>
> Thou'rt awa, awa, from the bursting spring time,
> Tho' o'er thy head its green boughs wave;
> The lambs are leaving their little foot-prints
> On the turf of thy new-made grave."

What gentleness and sweetness in these lines! One of her prose works, "Cats and Dogs," still holds its own as one of the minor classics of natural history.

Rev. Robert William Fraser, a Perthshire man, succeeded Rev. Dr. Guthrie in St. John's Church, Edinburgh, in 1847, and was a learned and eloquent divine and a diligent pastor. He found time to write all but one of a dozen of important works on divinity, history, physical and natural science. He was a solid man.

I must not omit William Fraser, the educational reformer who helped David Stow to carry out his training system for teachers in Scotland, and who later investigated Scottish education, and wrote an important book on the subject of which the results were afterwards embodied in legislation. He died in 1879.

Along with him may well be mentioned the late James Fraser, Bishop of Manchester, a very famous man from Forfarshire, one of the Frasers of Durris, of whom it has been said that there has not been in this generation a more simple or noble soul. He interests us especially for his work in education, and forms a connecting link between our school system and English educational reform, for he visited Canada and the United States in 1865, and drew up a report which his biographer, Thomas Hughes, calls "a superb, an almost unique piece of work." It was the basis of the Foster Act of 1870, by which enormous changes were introduced in the direction of the American system.

Worthy of being put by his side was Rev. Donald Fraser, D.D., who died two years ago, of whom we should hear more under the head of theology. He received part of his education in old Knox College, Toronto, and was pastor of the Coté Street Church, Montreal, from which he was called to Inverness, thence to London, England.

In my mass of material, I had almost forgotten Patrick Lord Fraser, who died only five years ago. He was a very great man of the law, one of Scotland's greatest, and wrote extensively on legal subjects.

The Frasers, however, were not all heavy writers. Many of us remember John Fraser, who met his death by accident in Ottawa in 1872. He was best known as "Cousin Sandy." He had been a chartist before coming to Canada. He was a tailor by trade, and laid aside the needle for that other sharp pointed instrument, the pen. Most of his work was controversial and sarcastic. Here is a sample of his rollicking verse, reminding one strongly of the Ingoldsby legends:

> "William Blyth was a scape-grace—as many boys are—
> Who with prudence and forethought was always at war;
> His genius was active; I've heard, or have read,
> That his grandma was nervous; his father was dead;
> And his mother, released from connubial vows,
> Brought home to her dwelling a second-hand spouse,
> Who gave her a heart, somewhat hard and obtuse,
> In exchange for her furniture ready for use.
> Now William like others, without leave would roam,
> And be absent when father the second came home;
> So he of the step, which step-father should be,
> Said 'To save the lad's *morals* we'll send him to sea.'"

The boy was confined in a water-cask for bad conduct.

> "And the wave cleared the deck of the vessel, and she
> Like one half 'seas over' rolled about in the sea.
> Then a shriek was heard, and the boatswain roar'd
> 'There's Bill and the tub gone overboard!'"

He floated to shore after an interview with a shark, a cow switched her tail against the tub, and Bill caught it while the cow fled, and wrecked the tub, but saved Bill's life, although he remained unconscious.

> "But was roused from his swoon by a beautiful Yankee
> Who brought dough-nuts and tea, it was genuine Twankay.
> An angel of light in the garb of humanity,
> And that garb of the Saxony's best superfine,
> What her countrymen term the 'real genuine.'
> Bill was charmed and concluded, with some show of reason,
> That to her annexation could never be treason."

And he was annexed in due time.

We have some poets still living, Gordon Fraser, John W. Fraser, and others; on them I must touch lightly. Gordon is a writer on "Lowland Lore," and writes good ballads of his own, like the one beginning:

> "'Twas an eerie nicht, an' the storm-cluds lower'd,
> An the lichtnin's glent was keen,
> An' the thunner roll'd, but nane were cower'd
> I' the clachan till-hous bien."

It is a fearsome ghost story well told.

John W. is a very charming writer. His ballad of the courtship of "Bell" is first-rate, and it begins:

> "Sin' Bell cam' to bide in our toun,
> The warl' has a' gaen ajee;
> She has turned a' the heads o' the men,
> And the women wi' envy will dea.
> O, but Bell's bonnie!
> Dink as a daisy is she;
> Her e'en are as bricht as the starnies
> That shine in the lift sae hie."

Such are some of our literary men, and they are very creditable specimens. I know that I have left out more than I have given. I have not said a word about all the

Frasers in Gaelic literature, whose name must be legion, because I cannot follow them in that language.

Our Clan has a good proportion of the literary in it, and I believe we are all literary critics. I never knew a Fraser yet who had not excellent literary taste and judgment. The reasons why more literature has not been produced is very clear to my mind, and depends on a prominent characteristic of the Clan—great modesty. This must be thrown aside if you are going to rush into literature. Many a Fraser has had it in him to produce the highest sort of literature, who from this cause has never written a line for the public. When the Clan succeeds in throwing off this defect, we may expect the production of literary works on a par with the best that has been written.

The reply to the toast of "Frasers in Theology" was entrusted to the REV. MUNGO FRASER, D.D., of Hamilton, who had to leave by train for home before this toast was reached. His reply summarised is as follows: " There are many clansmen who stand high in theology, if we be allowed to understand by that term the wider and more comprehensive sphere of work in the Church of Christ. In the memory of those who admire subjective writings of an extremely searching character, the name of the Rev. James Fraser, of Brea, will occupy an undying place. To those who give the highest rank among ministers to pulpit ability, the Frasers of Kirkhill, for three generations, will afford examples of eloquence and those gifts of oratorical power that appeal so irresistibly to the popular ear. By those who regard the administrative functions of the pastor as of importance, the name of Bishop Fraser, of Manchester, is justly esteemed, and in a less prominent, but not less important degree, the name of Dr. William Fraser, for a long period the senior clerk of the Presbyterian Church in Canada; and theological literature finds a writer of ability and copiousness in Dr. Donald Fraser, at one time of Montreal and afterwards of London, England. The Clan contributed a great many names to the roll of distinguished clergymen, men who, in their different spheres, rendered noble service to the cause of Christ. And among them are men, some of whose names have been mentioned by the Vice-chairman, of ability, of high character, whose personal influence over the people was strongly felt. In Canada the name of Fraser has an honored place among the ministers of the churches. They are doing their duty nobly and well, and if the names of some of them be not widely known outside of their own country, it must not be forgotten that a clergyman's best fame and best reward is his good name among those for whom he directly labors, and for whose welfare he gives his best endeavors. Did time permit, it would be comparatively easy to speak at length of those who have held their own in the theological sphere, but sufficient has probably been said to indicate that the Clan has done its duty in one of the most interesting and important fields of human effort open for the welfare of man.

The part of the toast dealing with "the Frasers in War," was replied to by MR. ALEXANDER FRASER (of Fraserfield, Glengarry). He said: After what we have heard of the Clan this evening we must come to the conclusion that it has always been distinguished for its military spirit, and I regret on that account, all the more, that the duty has fallen upon me to reply to the " Frasers in War." Not that I do not appreciate to the fullest extent that spirit which distinguished them and probably in no small degree share it, but I am not a man of words, and I feel I shall not be able, even in a small way, to do justice to this theme. Undoubtedly the military character of the Clan goes back to its very origin, for if the Frasers did come from Normandy, they must have been selected on account of their military ability, for those were the days when length and strength of arm and good generalship were the most valuable qualifications a man could possess. But, coming down to the earlier times in Scotland, we find our clansmen heading the warlike and chivalrous nobles of that country, in their devotion to the Crown, and in their exploits in the field in defence of country and patrimony. I need not enter into a detailed description of the times when the Lowland Frasers served their country and their king with an unswerving devotion whose lustre time will not dim, nor the researches of modern historians tarnish. Down through history in the Highlands they have ever shown themselves to be a brave and warlike race, furnishing individuals of conspicuous ability and distinction in arms. No treatment of this toast would be complete that should omit a reference to Fraser's Highlanders that embarked under the command of the Chief of the Clan in 1757, and took part with Wolfe's army in all the engagements, from Louisburg to the close of the war. At Quebec the Frasers distinguished themselves in an especial manner. In the struggles which took place early in the century, between the Canadians and Americans, the Frasers did their duty, proving that down to our own times they maintained their old reputation. In the British army, from the formation of the Highland regiments, in 1739, to the present day, the

Clan has given many distinguished officers and many brave men to its country's service, and I know I can speak with truth when I say that the old spirit still prevails, whether you look at home or abroad. So true is this that I may conclude these remarks in the stereotyped words of the after-dinner speaker by saying that should the occasion ever demand it, the Frasers will be ever ready to draw their claymores and shed their blood in the country's service as of yore.

Mr. W. P. Fraser spoke for "The Frasers in Politics." He said : Mr. Chairman, Vice-chairman and Brother Clansmen, it would seem that the toast of distinguished clansmen is quite an inexhaustible one. Much has been said of our clansmen in the various ranks of life, but I believe no more than is deserved. As a matter of course the Frasers have ranked high in politics. We have not had a Prime Minister of the name in the Dominion of Canada, but we have given to the Legislatures of Ontario, Quebec, and the Lower Provinces, many of their most useful members, their most eloquent speakers, and their most responsible statesmen. We have borne our share of public duty in this country, both in the rank and file of political workers, and as leaders. I do not need to g．．． afield to find some of the more striking exam．．． ．．． 1ere is one name so long and honorably associa． ．． ．． ．rtunes of this Province that it merits prem．． ．．．． I refer to that of the Hon. Christopher F ．． ．r, who would have responded to this toast himself to ．ught, were it not that he has been suffering from severe illness for some time, and has not sufficiently recovered to take his place among us. Reference has been made to his letter of regret, and I feel sure that every word in it is true—that it is the outcome of his sincere feeling ; for Mr. Fraser is as much a clansman as he is a politician, and has ever manifested the same deep interest in matters connected with his Clan, as he has displayed in the public duties which he is called upon to perform. The position which he occupies, the services which he has rendered, his wide sphere of influence, his sterling honesty and unblemished record—these lie as an open book before you. For me to expatiate upon them would be quite superfluous. His name will go down in the annals of our statesmen as one of the most competent Ministers of the Crown who ever held office in this Province, as one of subtle intellect who served his country and his party in great crises, as one who gave his talents generously and disinterestedly to the welfare of his fellow-beings, and in a peculiar manner helped to lay the foundations of a great nationality in this country. Another of our clansmen, whose telegram of regret shows that he has been intercepted on the way from the far east to our gathering, has made the name famous in the politics of Canada, and is likely to attain to still greater eminence in the future. At his home in Nova Scotia he has long been known as a man of probity, ability, and capacity for pub'   '. It is not so long ago that he was first heard of in   'ern parts, but already he has sprung into notice   ces are in request at many public gatherings   e all regret the absence of Mr. D. C. Fraser,   ,·sboro', to-night. He is not only a politician but ' a. ɔn of learning and celtic literature. To his generous heart and open hand many a struggling Highlander owes much, and through his encouragement not a few scholarly productions have seen the light of day. Were I to venture beyond Canada I should find Frasers playing a prominent part in the field of politics in South Africa, in the Australias, in the East Indies, and even in South America. It was only the other day we heard of a clansman born in Nova Scotia, but of good Inverness stock, who had been appointed delegate to the Inter-colonial Conference to be held in Ottawa this summer. I refer to the Hon. Simon Fraser, of Victoria. I have no doubt his clansmen here will be glad to welcome him, and to wish the utmost success to his mission. I must refrain at this hour from any reference to what Frasers have done in political life in the old land. The chiefs of the Clan numbered among them many men of eminence in politics. Of these we have heard something already to-night, and when the call of public duty comes, I feel sure a Fraser will be ready to step forward to perform his part in a worthy manner.

ORGANIZATION.

A resolution was carried in favor of the formation of an organization of clansmen in Canada, having for its main objects the promotion of social intercourse among the members, the collection of facts from which to prepare a biographical album of the members and other clansmen, and the promotion of objects which may be of interest to the Clan; and that those present form a general committee to act in the matter, the Committee of this gathering to act as an Executive Committee, for the purpose of drafting a constitution for the Clan to be submitted to the next gathering of the Clan.

The Clan song, composed by request, for this gathering, by Mrs. Georgina Fraser Newhall, and set to music composed by Mr. J. Lewis Browne, will be found, with a biographical sketch and portrait of the authoress, on pages 93 to 97.

GEORGINA FRASER NEWHALL.

AUTHORESS OF "FRASER'S DRINKING SONG."

"The Frasers of Stratherrick, where are they?" To this pensive question by Charles Fraser Mackintosh comes an oft echoed and lusty answer from many distant lands. Indeed the question is, "Where are they not?" for it is safe to say that there is no country where the English language to-day prevails, in which Stratherrick may not claim a son. Their new homes have not the historical charm of the old, but wherever the Frasers have gone, away from the home of their fathers, they have acquitted themselves well. A scion of a Stratherrick house was James George Fraser, who many years ago settled at Galt, Ontario. Like his brother Capt. Charles Fraser, now residing in Glasgow, Scotland, he was attached to a Highland regiment in his younger days, but withdrawing from the service, he came to Canada with his young wife, Christina MacLeod. At Galt was born a family of three sons, William, Charles and Andrew, and four daughters, Christina, Jessie, Elizabeth and Georgina, the youngest of whom is the subject of this brief sketch. On the maternal side her descent is traced from the families of Lochend and Braemore. Her great-grand parents were George Mackenzie, second son of John Mackenzie I. of Lochend (of the Gairloch family), and Christina, daughter of Captain Hector Munro of Braemore. George Mackenzie was a distinguished officer, and attained to the rank of Lieut.-Colonel of the famous Rosshire Buffs, the 78th Highlanders. His daughter Christina married Angus MacLeod of Banff with issue, two sons, Donald and George, and several daughters,

MRS. GEORGINA FRASER NEWHALL

of whom Christina, as already stated, married James G. Fraser of Galt, Ontario.

Georgina Fraser was born about the beginning of the sixties, and was educated in the public and high schools of her native town. After the death of her parents she removed to Toronto, and taking up the study of shorthand entered upon the life of an amanuensis and teacher of stenography. She taught large classes in the towns surrounding Toronto, and in Victoria University, when that institution was located at Cobourg. She was the first woman in Canada to adopt this profession as a means of self-support, and to her belongs the honor of adding a new vocation to those upon which Canadian women may enter. In addition to these duties Miss Fraser undertook journalistic work, and was the first lady writer in Toronto to conduct the department devoted to woman's interests, now so important a weekly feature in the great dailies in Canada.

In 1884, while occupying the important position of Assistant Secretary to General Manager Oakes of the Northern Pacific Railway at St. Paul, Minn., she became the wife of Mr. E. P. Newhall, of the Pacific Express Co. in Omaha.

Notwithstanding household cares and ill-health Mrs. Newhall still finds time to indulge in her old taste for literature, wielding an earnest pen in advocacy of those reforms which most interest women of advanced thought. She has achieved considerable fame as a writer of short stories, and her compositions of verse bear the mark of the true poet's touch.

As a clanswoman Mrs. Newhall is fond of claiming the right to call herself a "black" Fraser, nature having endowed her with that darkness of hair and eyebrow which is supposed to stamp all the possessors thereof as "true Frasers."

FRASER'S DRINKING SONG.

1

All ready?
    Let us drink to the woman who rules us to-night —
    To her lands; to her laws; 'neath her flag we will smite
Ev'ry foe,
Hip and thigh,
Eye for eye,
Blow for blow—
        Are you ready?

2

All ready?
    Then here's to the mothers who bore us, my men;
    To the shieling that sleeps in the breast of the glen
Where the stag
Drinks it fill
From the rill
By the crag—
        Are you ready?

3

All ready?
    Fill your glass to the maid you adore, my boys;
    Wish her health, wish her wealth, long life, and all joys;
Full measure
(May it swim
To the brim)
Of pleasure—
        Are you ready?

4

All ready?
    And here's to the country we live in, my lads;
    It is here we have struggled and thriven, my lads?
God bless it,
May Beauty
And Duty
Possess it—
        Are you ready?

5

All ready?
    A Fraser! A Fraser forever, my friends;
    While he lives how he hates, how he loves till life ends;
He is first,
Here's my hand,
Into grand
Hurrah burst—
        Are you ready?

SIMON FRASER.

DISCOVERER OF THE FRASER RIVER.

The life-work of the discoverer of the Fraser River illustrates the pioneer spirit which animated the early settlers of Canada. There was the pluck, the love of adventure, the endurance, the prompt response to the call of duty, the expansive idea which kept abreast of ever opening possibilities, and the rare tact displayed in new, embarrassing and important transactions. Simon Fraser was in many respects a great man and one of whom his clansmen may well feel proud. His grandfather was William Fraser, of Culbokie, whose wife Margaret Macdonell, of Glengarry, was the possessor of the famous *Balg Solair* in which was stowed away a manuscript of Ossianic poetry, which figures in the dissertations on the authenticity of MacPherson's Ossian, and regarding which the following interesting passage occurs in the correspondence of the late Bishop Alexander Macdonell: "I myself saw a large MS. of Ossian's poems in the possession of Mrs. Fraser of Culbokie, in Strathglass, which she called *"am Balg Solair"* (a bag of fortuitous goods). This lady's residence being between my father's house and the school where I used to attend with her grandchildren, at her son's, Culbokie House, by way of coaxing me to remain on cold nights at her own house, she being cousin to my father, she used to take up the *Balg Solair*, and read pieces of it to me. Although a very young boy at the time, I became so much enraptured with the rehearsal of the achievements of the heroes of the poem, and so familiar with the characters, especially of Oscar, Cathmor, and Cuthchullin, that when MacPherson's translation was put into my hands in the Scotch college of Valladolid in Spain, many years afterwards, it was like meeting old friends with whom I had been intimately acquainted. Mrs. Fraser's son, Simon, who had a classical education, and was an excellent Gaelic scholar, on emigrating to America in the year 1774, took the *Balg Solair* with him as an invaluable treasure. On the breaking out of the Revolutionary war, Mr. Fraser joined the Royal Standard, was taken prisoner by the Americans and thrown into jail, where he died."

William, of Culbokie, and his wife Margaret Macdonell had nine sons. Of these, Archibald and John fought under Wolfe at Quebec. John settled at Montreal, and became Chief Justice of the Montreal district. In 1774, or more probably in 1773, Simon left home, and settled near Bennington, Vermont. Here his son, the subject of this sketch, was born in 1776. His mother and her family came to Canada after the death of his father (as stated above), and settled in Glengarry. Simon was the youngest of the family. He was placed in school in Montreal, where he resided with his uncle, the Chief Justice. In 1792, at the age of sixteen, he became an articled clerk with McTavish, Frobisher & Co., to the North-West Fur Trading Co., which had its headquarters in Montreal. In 1802 he became a partner, and subsequently went out to the far North. In 1805 he came down from Fort Athabasca to Fort William, and was then nominated to cross the Rocky Mountains, to extend out-posts and form trading connections with the Indians. He responded at once to the call. He said he would undertake the expedition provided they gave him a sufficient outfit. This the Company were only too glad to do. It was a very hazardous undertaking. He crossed the mountains with thirty men—clerks, axemen, guides and interpreters. He soon found himself in a wild and desolate region. As he went on he built block-houses, and took possession of the country in the name of the King. In 1806 he discovered the river which takes its name from him. He discovered many rivers and lakes which he named after different members of the Company. He traced the Fraser river to its source, and met many different tribes of Indians, some friendly, others hostile. At one time they met different tribes who were very friendly and made a great feast for them ; they killed their *fattest dog* for him, which of course he feigned to eat ; but at the same feast the chiefs held a council and decided to put him to death, which the interpreter, who understood their language, told him, and they stole quietly away. He first named the river now known as the Fraser river, the "Great River," and called the place "New Caledonia." Here he left some of the party, and crossed westerly into the open country, and built another house near a ake, which he called Fraser's Lake. He was now with four men in the midst of Indians who had never before either seen or heard of the "pale face." On the border of this lake he witnessed an Indian ceremony. He was brought by the Indians to where they had a large burying-ground, where one of the Chiefs of their tribe was being buried. An immense number of warriors were assembled, and after a most solemn and impressive ceremony, Mr. Fraser was invited by signs to approach the grave. He did so, and gave immense satisfaction by engraving his name on a post which had been planted over the remains of the departed warrior. In July, 1807, he received fresh supplies from the North-West Co., who at the same time urged him to trace with all possible speed the "Great River" to the Sea, they being apprehensive that the Americans would get ahead of the British in that quarter, as in the previous year 1806, Captains Lewis and Clarke had gone down the "Columbia," and were extending American authority along the western coast of America, and Astor, on the part of the Americans, was also looking anxiously towards the northern section.

The North-West Co. therefore urged Mr. Fraser to spare no expense in achieving the object of their desires.

Mr. Fraser built another trading-house on the "Great River" in 1807, and reached the Ocean in July, 1808. He remained but a short time there on account of the hostility of the Indians.

Returning he again met numerous and large bodies of Indians speaking several different languages. They assembled to see the wonderful pale faces who had come among them. An idea of how they regarded white men may be formed from the fact that when hundreds of them were congregated together, at the discharge of a single rifle they would fall prostrate on the ground, so great was their astonishment. Had it not been for Mr. Fraser's wonderful energy and enterprise, there would not be a railroad to-day from ocean to ocean over British territory.

SIMON, LORD LOVAT.

BEHEADED ON TOWER HILL.

No Fraser chief has achieved more notoriety than Simon, the fourteenth Lord Lovat. His enemies avenged themselves for the failure of their nefarious plots against him by supplying, at a cheap rate, the charcoal with which prejudiced historians have blackened his memory. But while his fate is still held up as a warning to evil doers, it has been proved, beyond peradventure, that his character has been much maligned, and that he appears rather as a man of inexhaustible resources, availing himself of whatever means lay nearest to his hand to extricate himself from enormous difficulties and to attain objects which, though of personal advantage to himself and Clan, were as honorable as they were just, and wholly in keeping with the customs of his day. His efforts to secure the chiefship and the honors of his house, and to extend the power of the Clan, were genuinely patriotic. His Lordship certainly was a man of learning and ability. He was an admirable letter writer, and passages in his correspondence show that he had wonderful facility in writing and a capital style.

The picture here given is from a mezzo-tint in possession of Mr. B. Homer Dixon, from a painting of Lord Lovat, by David Le Clerc, a Swiss who was in England in 1715 and 1716. The picture which is supposed to have been taken in 1715, when Lord Lovat was about forty-eight years old, is marked: "Le Clare, *pinxt*. J. Simon, *fecit*." Although armour had been disused before Lord Lovat's time, it was the fashion at that period for gentlemen to be painted in armour. The mezzo-tint is very rare.

BRIGADIER SIMON FRASER.

Among the officers of Fraser's Highlanders were several clansmen destined to rise high in military distinction. Of them few are better known in the Clan than Captain Simon Fraser of Balnain, afterwards Quarter-Master General in Ireland, a post which he quitted to serve as Brigadier-General in Burgoyne's Army in America. He had served in the Scotch regiment in the Dutch service, and was wounded at Bergen-op-Zoom. He spoke French perfectly and to this accomplishment and his coolness was due his signal service at Quebec, where he saved the transports from discovery at a critical moment before the precipice was scaled.

Smollet relates the incident as follows :—"The French had posted sentries along shore to challenge boats and vessels and give the alarm occasionally. The first boat that contained the English troops being questioned accordingly, a captain of Fraser's regiment, who had served in Holland, and who was perfectly well acquainted with the French language and customs, answered without hesitation to *qui vive ?*—which is their challenging word—*La France* ; nor was he at a loss to answer the second question, which was much more particular and difficult. When the sentinel demanded, *a quel regiment ?* the captain replied, *de la reine*, which he knew by accident to be one of those that composed the body commanded by Bougainville. The soldier took it for granted this was the expected convoy (a convoy of provisions expected that night for the garrison of Quebec), and, saying *passe*, allowed all the boats to proceed without further question. In the same manner the other sentries were deceived; though one, more wary than the rest, came running down to

BRIGADIER-GENERAL FRASER,
YOUNGER OF BALNAIN.

the water's edge and called, *pour quoi est ce que vous ne parlez pas haut?* 'Why don't you speak with an audible voice?' To this interrogation, which implied doubt, the captain answered with admirable presence of mind, in a soft tone of voice, *tai toi nous serens entendues!* 'Hush! we shall be overheard and discovered.' Thus cautioned the sentry retired without further altercation."

At the time of the Revolutionary War, Brigadier-General Simon Fraser was second in command of the British army, under Burgoyne. He fell at Saratoga under circumstances which prove his great ability as an officer. The American historians say that General Burgoyne had lost his head, and the American General Morgan perceiving it, called two of his best riflemen and said : " You see that fine fellow on the white horse? It goes against my heart to do it, but you must pick him off, or we lose the battle." They watched their opportunity, shot General Fraser, and the Americans won the day.

The picture here given is said to be a good likeness. It has been produced from a mezzo-tint in the possession of Mr. B. Homer Dixon, Toronto.

SECOND ANNUAL GATHERING.

*"Three triumphs in a day ; three hosts subdued in one :
Three armies scattered like the spray, beneath one common sun."*

THE second Annual Gathering and Dinner of the Clan Fraser in Canada was held on the 25th day of February, 1895, that date having been selected in honor of the Scots' victory at Roslin on February 25th, 1303, when the army was commanded by Sir Simon Fraser, the patriot (p. 48). The place of meeting was the Rossin House, Toronto. The gentlemen were accompanied by lady friends, a departure from the custom generally observed on similar festive occasions, that contributed greatly to the pleasure of the evening. The committee in charge of the arrangements was composed of Dr. J. B. Fraser (Chairman of Programme Committee), Professor W. H. Fraser, Messrs. G. B. Fraser, R L. Fraser, Alexander Fraser (Fraserfield), Alexander R. Fraser, W. P. Fraser, Andrew Fraser, Alexander Fraser (MacFhionnlaidh), Chairman ; and W. A. Fraser, Secretary. Those present were Rev. Dr. Mungo Fraser, Hamilton ; Mr. W. Lewis Fraser, New York ; Mr. Donald Fraser. Kingston ; Mr. R. I. Fraser, Barrie ; Mr. Andrew Fraser, Barrie ; Messrs. Robert Lovat Fraser, George B. Fraser, and Miss Fraser ; Professor W. H. Fraser and Mrs. Fraser ; Dr. J. B. Fraser and Mrs. Fraser ; Alexander Fraser (Fraserfield), Mrs. Fraser and Miss Kate Fraser ; Alexander R. Fraser and Mrs. Fraser ; Alexander Fraser (MacFhionnlaidh), Mrs. Fraser, Miss Fraser, Mrs. Georgina Fraser-Newhall, and Mrs. Ramsay ; Mr. W. A. Fraser and Mrs. Fraser ; Dr. Pyne and Mrs. Pyne ; Alexander Fraser

(Parkdale), and Miss Fraser ; W. P. Fraser, Donald Fraser, Charles Fraser, Mrs. C. G. Fraser and Master Norman Fraser, James Fraser, Henry Sandham Fraser.

Letters of regret at their inability to attend were read from Messrs. E. A. Fraser, Detroit ; D. Fraser, Montreal ; Ex-Mayor Fraser, Petrolea ; O. K. Fraser, Brockville ; A. Fraser, Hamilton ; P. M. Fraser, St. Thomas ; Rev. R. D. Fraser, Bowmanville ; and Rev. Dr. J. B. Fraser, Annan.

Mr. Alexander Fraser (MacFhionnlaidh) presided, and the vice-chairs were occupied by Messrs. George B. Fraser and R. L. Fraser, and Mr. W. A. Fraser acted as Secretary.

The after-dinner programme was interesting and varied. Besides the usual toasts it included the "Fraser's Drinking Song," composed by Mrs. Georgina Fraser-Newhall, and sung by Mrs. Alexander Fraser ; readings by Prof. W. H. Fraser, bagpipe selections by Pipe-Major MacSwayed, and Highland dancing by Master Norman Fraser.

The speeches contained a great deal of information regarding the Clan, and were very interesting. Most eloquent was the speech delivered by Mr. W. Lewis Fraser, of New York, who entered into the history of the Clan at considerable length ; and that by Mrs. Georgina Fraser-Newhall, in response to the toast of her health.

A group photograph was successfully taken of the company by the aid of a flash-light, which will remain a memento of a very pleasant gathering.

Before dispersing the report of the Committee on the Organization of the Clan was read. It set forth that meetings had been held at which the Clan had been organized, and the annexed Constitution and By-laws prepared :

THE CLAN FRASER IN CANADA.

(*Instituted May 5th, 1894.*)

CONSTITUTION AND BY-LAWS.

ARTICLE I.—NAME.—The name of this organization shall be : "The Clan Fraser in Canada."

ARTICLE II.—OBJECTS.—The objects of the Clan shall be :

The cultivation of friendly intercourse and social relations among those bearing the surname "Fraser," and the promotion among its members of love for the Clan, and increased interest in its history and traditions :

The collection of Clan records, traditions and anecdotes ; of documents bearing upon the Clan history ; of information relating to notable clansmen, especially with reference to the early history of the Clan in Canada ; and the compilation of an album of portraits and biographical sketches of Clansmen in Canada :

The furtherance of the interests of clansmen, whether in Scotland or in Canada, and the giving of such assistance to clansmen in need as may be within the power of the Clan.

ARTICLE III.—MEMBERSHIP.—Persons bearing the surname "Fraser," by birth or by marriage, shall be eligible for membership in the Clan. Honorary membership may be conferred on distinguished clansmen, or on persons, not clansmen, who have rendered conspicuous service to the Clan.

ARTICLE IV.—ARMS, MOTTO AND BADGE.—The arms of the Clan Fraser in Canada shall be the same as those of the Clan proper, with the difference of a wreath of Canadian maple leaves intertwined (a fac-simile of which is impressed on this Constitution) ; the "Motto" and "Badge" shall be that of the Clan Fraser—motto, "Ju Suis Prest" ; badge, a sprig of yew—*Taxus Baccata*.

ARTICLE V.—(*a*) EXECUTIVE OFFICERS.—The Executive Officers shall consist of a Chief, Chieftains (as hereinunder provided for), Secretary-Treasurer, Historians, Curator, and a Bard.

(*b*)—TRUSTEES AND COUNCILLORS.—There shall be three Trustees, six Councillors, a Pipe-Major and Pipers.

(*c*)—HONORARY CHIEF AND CHIEFTAINS.—The Chief of the Clan Fraser, "Mac-Shimi," shall be the Honorary Chief, and Honorary Chieftainship may be bestowed on clansmen who merit very high clan honor.

ARTICLE VI.—GATHERINGS.—The Clan shall gather once a year, on a day to be decided upon by the Executive Committee, for the transaction of business. That gathering shall be known as the Annual Business Meeting of the Clan. On the evening of the same day a Clan Dinner, or other form of Entertainment, shall take place.

ARTICLE VII.—At the Annual Business Meeting of the Clan the Executive Officers, Trustees, Councillors and Pipers, Honorary Chief (when vacant), and Honorary Chieftains (when Honorary Chieftainship is conferred), shall be elected ; and the roll of members, prepared by the Executive Committee, shall be revised.

ARTICLE VIII.—The principle upon which Chieftains and Councillors shall be elected shall be as follows : The Province of Ontario shall be divided into five Districts, viz. : Ottawa, Kingston, Toronto, Hamilton and London, from each of which and from each of the other Provinces of Canada, a Chieftain shall be elected. A Chieftain may be also elected from each of the States of the American Union, as an interest in the Clan may be manifested. The Ontario Districts shall comprise the following counties :

OTTAWA.—Glengarry, Prescott, Stormont, Dundas, Grenville, Carleton, Russell, Renfrew.

KINGSTON.—Addington, Lennox, Frontenac, Hastings, Prince Edward, Leeds, Lanark.

TORONTO.—Northumberland, Peterborough, Haliburton, Victoria, Durham, Ontario, Muskoka, Parry Sound, Nipissing, York, Peel, Toronto.

HAMILTON.—Wentworth, Lincoln, Welland, Brant, Waterloo, Simcoe, Dufferin, Grey, Wellington, Halton.

LONDON.—Middlesex, Elgin, Oxford, Norfolk, Haldimand, Kent, Lambton, Essex, Bruce, Huron, Perth.

There shall be at least one Councillor elected to represent each District in Ontario.

ARTICLE IX.—The Executive Officers, Trustees and Councillors shall form a General Committee, which shall prepare the business for the Annual Meeting. The Executive Officers shall form the Executive Committee of the General Committee. The General Committee and the Executive Committee may appoint Sub-Committees with power to transact business on behalf of the Clan.

ARTICLE X.—DUTIES OF OFFICERS.—The CHIEF shall preside at all the meetings of Committees, at the Annual Business Meeting, and at the Annual Entertainment of the Clan ; in his absence the duties of the Chief shall devolve upon the CHIEFTAINS in order of seniority, and in the absence of all of them the clansmen present shall elect a Chairman *pro tem*. The SECRETARY-TREASURER shall keep a correct minute of the business transacted at the meetings of Committees and at the Annual Meeting of the Clan ; he shall keep a roll of the membership of the Clan ; with the Chief he shall convene the meetings, and shall conduct the correspondence and general business of the Clan ; he shall submit his accounts to an audit annually or on the demand of the Executive Committee. The HISTORIANS shall compile the Clan Album, and shall edit any papers containing information regarding the Clan or clansmen which may be secured for the Clan. The CURATOR shall have the custody of all property belonging to the Clan, including papers and books not in use by the proper officers, and shall account for the same to the TRUSTEES in whom the property shall be vested on behalf of the Clan, and who shall submit a report of their stewardship to the Annual Meeting of the Clan.

ARTICLE XI.—The roll of membership shall be compiled by the Executive Committee, and shall be subject to revision at the Annual Business Meeting.

ARTICLE XII.—The officers shall wear insignia of office ; and an officer holding the same office for three terms (not necessarily consecutively) shall become the possessor of the insignia as his own property.

ARTICLE XIII.—The Constitution and By-laws may be altered or amended at the Annual Business Meeting of the Clan, by a two-thirds vote of the membership, personally or by mandate; but notice of any such alteration of amendment in specific terms must be lodged with the Secretary-Treasurer at least two months before the date of the Annual Business Meeting so that members may be notified when the announcement of the Annual Business Meeting shall be made.

BY-LAWS.

1. The fee of membership shall be one dollar annually for gentlemen, and the sum of fifty cents for ladies and minors.

2. The Annual Meeting of the Clan shall be held on a date to be decided upon by the Executive Committee. ; in deciding upon the date, however, the convenience of the greatest number of the membership shall be the chief consideration.

3. Twelve members shall constitute a quorum for the transaction of business at the Annual Meeting.

4. A member may be expelled from the Clan for a transgression of any of its rules, or any other sufficient cause. Notice of intended expulsion must be given to the Secretary-Treasurer, who shall lay it before the Executive Committee for report at the Annual Business Meeting, and to the member whom it is proposed to expel. Voting shall be by ballot, and a majority must vote "yea" before a member can be expelled. The annual revision of the roll of membership referred to in the Constitution, Article XI., shall in no way be understood to imply expulsion from membership.

5. The following shall be the order of business : 1st. Reading of minutes of previous meeting ; 2nd. Reading of communications and action thereon ; 3rd. Unfinished business of previous meeting ; 4th, New business ; 5th. Election of officers ; 6th. Adjournment.

Signed on behalf of the Committee.

ALEXANDER FRASER, *Chairman*.   W. A. FRASER, *Secretary*.

The above Constitution and By-laws were duly adopted and ordered to be printed.

THE OFFICERS.

The following Officers were elected for the term 1895-'96:

Honorary Chief,
LORD LOVAT.

Honorary Chieftain,
MR. CHARLES FRASER MACKINTOSH, Inverness

Chief,
MR. ALEX. FRASER (MACFHIONNLAIDH), Toronto.

Chieftains,
District of Ottawa : MR. ALEX. FRASER, Westmeath.
Kingston : MR. DONALD FRASER, Kingston.
Toronto : MR. G. B. FRASER, Toronto.
Hamilton : REV. DR. MUNGO FRASER, Hamilton.
London : EX-MAYOR FRASER, Petrolea.

Provinces—Maritime Provinces : D. C. FRASER, M. P., NewGlasgow, N.S.
Quebec : MR. DONALD FRASER, Montreal.
Northwest Territories : MR. J. G. FRASER, Regina, N.W.T.
British Columbia : MR. W. FRASER, Vancouver, B.C.

State of Michigan : MR. E. A. FRASER, Detroit, U.S.A.
New York : MR. W. LEWIS FRASER, New York.

Councillors,
Ottawa : MR. A. W. FRASER, Ottawa.
Kingston : MR. O. K. FRASER, Brockville.
Toronto { MR. ALEX. FRASER (Fraserfield), Toronto.
{ DR. J. B. FRASER, Toronto.
Hamilton : MR. R. I. FRASER, Barrie.
London : MR. WM. FRASER, of Port Stanley.

Secretary-Treasurer,
Mr. W. A. FRASER, Toronto.

Chaplain,
REV. DR. MUNGO FRASER, Hamilton.

Historians,
PROF. W. H. FRASER and MR. ALEX. FRASER, Toronto.

Curator,
Mr. ALEXANDER FRASER, Toronto.

Trustees,
MESSRS. R. L. FRASER, Toronto ; ABNER FRASER, Hamilton ; A. G. FRASER, London.

Bard,
GEORGINA FRASER-NEWHALL, Omaha.